Harmonisation
of laws in Africa

Malthouse Law Books
portable edition

Egweike, K. I., *Agency*
Egweike, K. I., *Hire Purchase*
Egweike, K. I., *Sale of Goods*
Ola, C. S., *Law of Contract with Nigerian companies*
John Ademola Yakubu, *Limits to the application of foreign laws*

Harmonisation of laws in Africa

By

Dr John Ademola Yakubu
LL.B(Hons); B.L; LL.M; Ph.D
Reader, Faculty of Law
University of Ibadan, Ibadan, Nigeria
and
Honourable Attorney-General and
Commissioner for Justice
of Oyo State of Nigeria

ℳℙ

MALTHOUSE PRESS LTD

First published 1999 by Malthouse Press Ltd.

Copyright © 1999 John Ademola Yakubu

2nd Imprint 2004

Malthouse Press Ltd.
8, Amore Street, off Toyin Street, Ikeja,
PO Box 500 Ikeja, Lagos State, Nigeria
Email: malthouse_lagos@yahoo.co.uk

Lagos, Benin, Ibadan, Jos, Oxford, Port-Harcourt, Zaria

Distributed outside Africa by:
African Books Collective
www.africanbookscollective.com
abc@africanbookscollective.com

ISBN 9780230955

Printed by Lightning Source

Dedication

To my late sister Nike.

Preface

Notwithstanding the sovereignty of various countries, the need for legal cooperation among the various countries of the world cannot be over-emphasised.

One viable method of bringing about international co-operation is through the harmonisation of laws. The need for this approach arose a long time ago. So many bodies or institutions are now in existence for the purpose of achieving uniformity in the operation of the laws of various states. Such institutions include the Hague Conference on Private International Law, the Unidroit, the Uncitral, the EEC and the Council of Europe. The advantages derivable from this method are emphasised in this book.

Of particular importance and relevance is the appreciation of this idea in Africa. There are regional bodies like the ECOWAS, the East African Community, the SADC and the PTA. A giant step at continental level is the emergence of the African Economic Treaty. This body serves as the umbrella body at the continental level for the purpose of harmonisation of laws in Africa.

This work is a bold attempt to put in focus the idea of harmonisation and the journey so far in Africa. This work also contains valuable information on harmonisation efforts outside Africa.

Dr John Ademola Yakubu
Reader, Faculty of Law, University of Ibadan, Ibadan
and Honourable Attorney General and Commissioner for Justice,
Ibadan, Oyo State.

Acknowledgements

This work is the outcome of my research at the School of Law, Kings College, London where I worked for one session- October 1995 to July 1996. My one year sojourn at the School of Law, Kings College, London was facilitated by the Association of Commonwealth Universities having been granted a Commonwealth Scholarship. I am indebted to the British Council for the sponsorship.

I worked with Professor C. G. J.Morse who is now the Head of School at Kings College, School of Law, London and one of the editors of that authoritative book on conflict of Laws--``Dicey and Morris on the Conflict of Laws.'' He made his library available to me and he carefully enriched my knowledge of this technical area of the Law. I hereby acknowledge my indebtedness to him. I am also grateful to Professor Ian Kennedy, then Head of School of Law. He provided me with an office and saw to my needs. Indeed, I am grateful to all the members of staff of the School of Law, Kings College both Administrative and Academic, for all they did to make me happy in England. I thank Mr Emile Yakpo for his friendship. I thank Honourable Justice Abdul Koroma and Prince Bola Ajibola of the International Court of Justice, the Hague, Netherlands for the interraction I had with them in South Africa.

I must put on record my appreciation to Professor 'Wale Omole, the Vice Chancellor of the Obafemi Awolowo university, Ile-Ife who recommended me for the scholarship. I thank Professor J. O. Fabunmi, Professor (Mrs) Okorodudu Fubara, Dr. A. O. Popoola and other members of staff of the Obafemi Awolowo University, Ile-Ife where I was when I got the scholarship for their support. I thank Mr Bolaji Owasanoye for providing me with useful information on AET. I must mention the name of Prof. I. O. Agbede who is a mentor to me. I thank him for his usual useful advice. I also thank Professor Fola Shyllon, Prof

J. D. Ojo, Prof. J.O. Anifalaje and other members of staff of the University of Ibadan for being worthy colleagues. I thank Prof. O. Adewoye, the Vice Chancellor of the University of Ibadan for his support.

I must also put on record my appreciation to the Military Administrator of Oyo State, Compol Prince Amen Oyakhire for his support. The same goes for Mr Adebisi Adesola, the Secretary to the State Government and Head of Service and my fellow Commissioners. I must also register my appreciation to Col. A. Usman, who appointed me the Attorney General and Commissioner for Justice of the State when he was the Military Administrator.

I thank my junior ones for their help at various times. This work is dedicated to my late junior sister-Nike Ogundepo (nee Yakubu). May her gentle soul rest with the Lord.

I thank the Publishers for publishing this work.

Dr. John Ademola Yakubu
Honourable Attorney General and Commissioner for Justice
Ministry of Justice,
Secretariat, Ibadan.
22nd January, 1999.

Contents

1.1 Nature of the Subject
1.2 Question of Nomenclature
1.3 History of Private International Law
1.4 Developments in Some Continental Countries
    1.4.1 The French School
    1.4.2 The Dutch Authors
1.5. English Private International Law
1.6. The Development of American conflict of Laws
1.7. The German Scholars
1.8. Mancini
1.9. Nigeria

2.1 Problems of Harmonisation of Private International Law the developing
countries

3.1. The Hague Conference on Private International Law
3.2. Organisation and process of harmonisation by the Hague Conference
3.3 International Institute for the Uunification of Private Law (Unidroit)
3.4. The Council of Europe
3.5 The European Economic Community (EEC)
3.6 The Legislative Power of the Community

Table of cases

1

Nature and history of private international law

Nature of the subject

The economic and social affairs of men have never been restricted to the units which they erect to administer their law and government. Thus, men in their love for adventure and in their curiosity to discover places hitherto unknown had interacted over the years beyond their nation boundaries culminating in the need to formulate rules to govern everyday activities beyond the accidental geographical bounds. The need to have well defined rules to regulate activities beyond state bounds gave rise to the recognition of private international law. To put it in another way, it has been realised that no nation, so to speak, is an Island, necessitating the need for co-operation among various peoples and nation-states. An outstanding characteristic of this subject however is the lack of consensus in respect of its methods and goals. As it has been rightly pointed out, the uncertainty about the proper approach to multistate problems reigns supreme and the conceptual apparatus of the approaches that have been proposed is as complex as it is unconvincing.[1] Dean Prosser put the problem in focus when he wrote.

> The realms of the conflict of laws is a dismal swamp filled with quaking quagmires, and inhabited by learned but eccentric professors who theorise about mysterious matters in a strange and incomprehensive jargon.[2]

The complex nature of the subject stems from the fact that it is all embracing in the sense that it deals with any problem, no matter its nature, where there is a conflict of issue or where there is an indication

---

[1] Juenger F., *Choice of Law and Multistate Justice* p. 1.
[2] Prosser, ``Interstate Publication" (1953) 51 *Mich. L. Rev.* 959 at 971

that the legal systems of two or more countries may be involved in the determination of a particular issue before the court. It could therefore be said that private international law is not a separate branch of law in the same sense as, say, the law of contract or tort. It is an all-pervading subject. One would therefore agree with Harrison when he said:

> It (private international law) starts up unexpectedly in any court and in the midst of any process. It may spring like a mine in a plain common law action, in an administrative proceeding in equity, or in a divorce case, or a bankruptcy case, in a shipping case or a matter of criminal procedure... The most trivial action of debt, the most complex case of equitable claims, may be suddenly interrupted by the appearance of a knot to be untied only by private international law.[3]

Despite this complexity, a given conflict problem usually involves three basic issues viz:

(i)   Jurisdiction

(ii) choice of law and

(iii) Recognition and enforcement of judgements.

Jurisdiction raises the question whether the local court, or in conflicts terminology, the forum court can hear a case before it. The issue of jurisdiction where a foreign element is in issue raises therefore the competence of the forum court to adjudicate having regard to the existence of a non-local element or elements and the question whether even if it is competent, it is reasonable in the circumstance to do so. If the court is satisfied that it has jurisdiction and that it is appropriate for it to do so, it will then proceed to determine the controversy between the parties.

After jurisdiction must have been assumed, the court will have to decide whether the local law ought to be applied or whether given the foreign nature of the transaction or the agreement of the parties it must defer to a foreign rule of decision. The choice of law process may assume a complex dimension in some cases. For example in the area of

---

[3] Harrison, T. *Jurisprudence and the Conflict of Laws* p.101

family law, the *lex fori* is favoured but in others like contracts, torts and property, reference may be made to foreign law. Furthermore, the English law allocates *lex domicilii* to the essential validity of a marriage and *lex loci celebrationis* in respect of formal validity. American law refers to the *lex loci celebrationis* in both cases. The choice of law to govern an issue may therefore affect the outcome of the case before the court. It could therefore be said that the question which state's law should be applied must ultimately rest on some rational approach which itself is inextricably bound up with the very fundamental question as regards the reason for the failure of the local court to depart from its own domestic rules of decision.[4]

The judgement of a foreign court may be relied upon in a domestic litigation. The foreign judgement may constitute an estoppel, the consequence of which is the preclusion of litigation of a matter decided by the foreign court. A foreign judgement may also constitute a defence to a subsequent suit brought by the plaintiff in the forum. And, of course, a plaintiff who has succeeded in a suit may seek to enforce the judgement in the forum. It may also justify the staying of a similar action in the forum to avoid a multiplicity of litigation. The issue of recognition and enforcement of judgements is therefore of paramount importance in private international law.

Question of nomenclature

Two names are often used interchangeably to describe this subject. The first is 'conflict of laws'[5] while the other is 'private international law.[6] There is no consensus as regards which is to be preferred. Critics of the term "conflict of laws" argue that it implies that some sort of trial of strength takes place between contesting legal systems to determine

---

[4] Sykes & Pryles, *International and Interstate Conflict of Law* (2nd Ed. 1981) p. 3

[5] This name is preferred in America. This name is attributable to Rodenburg.

[6] Story is said to have coined this name. This is the name preferred in the United Kingdom.

which one applies to a particular dispute whereas there is no such contest, since the basic aim is to choose the better or appropriate, rather than the strongest legal system.

As regards private international law, it has been said that the use of "international" in the name of the subject confuses issues and makes this subject look like public international law.[7] It seems however that this is a tenuous argument. This is because whereas public international law is essentially an area of the law dealing with legal relations between states, private international law is a branch of the legal system of each nation which regulates legal relations between states, each legal system has its own idea of private international law. It is therefore fashionable to talk of English private international law, French private international law or Nigerian private international law. The objection as regards the use of the word "international" seems misplaced because the reason for its adoption is to describe the ideal of the possibility of adopting the legal system of another nation in the resolution of a legal problem.[8] For this reason, it seems that this purpose is being served and the subject may appropriately be labelled "private international law".

History of private international law

It is ideal to start with the early Roman Empire. The state of affairs in the early Roman Empire paved the way for an early recognition of private international law. The existence of a number of urban communities gave rise to conflicting territorial laws. Italy, Rome excepted, was made up of a large number of towns, then known as *municipia* while the rest of the Empire was divided into separate provinces.[9] The connection of every inhabitant was either to Rome or one of the urban communities. The facultative element was either citizenship or domicil. Since citizenship resulted from Origo, adoption,

---

[7] See for example Spiro, *Conflict of Laws* (1973) p. 2. See Juenger F. K. ``Private International Private Law" 5 *K. C. J.* 45-at 45-46.
[8] There seems to be no argument in this regard.
[9] Savigny V., *The Conflict of Laws* (Guthrie's Transl.) S. 351 p. 45

manurisation or election, it was possible for a person to be a citizen of several urban communities at the same time. The Origo of each person was determined by the place of his father while that of an illegitimate was its mother.[10] This idea has survived up till today as the domicile of origin of a child in all patrilenial societies is that of connection with an urban community which has been freely chosen as the permanent abode and thus the centre of that person's legal relations and business. This was constituted by residence in a place with the intention of making the stay permanent.

The system of personal law became prominent with the fall of the Roman Empire. Personal law as opposed to territorial law became the prima facie law although each tribe retained its tribal laws. Criminal law and Canon law, however, were of universal application.[11] Issues like tutelage of women, dowry and the extent of a husband's authority became subject to rules of general application.[12]

The turn of the eleventh century saw the emergence of feudal units again. A direct negation of personality. Thus, a vassal to a feudal overlord was no longer amenable to his personal law, he was merely a man of his Lord and subject to this Lord's law. The consequence was that under this system, all laws, except those of the feudal overlord were disregarded, and any right acquired under such a different system was regarded as extraneous. This position was confined to the north of the Alps.

In the South of the Alps however, there was a substitution of territoriality for personality, for as it were, there emerged the existence of the growth of the Italian cities. The bond of the union between men in Italy was neither race nor subjection to a common feudal overlord, but residence in the city. At this time, a large number of prosperous cities like Bologna, Modena, Milan and Padua had begun to emerge. These were cities having their own territories as well as laws which were at variance with the generally prevailing Roman law. This diversity of

---

[10] Gibbon, *Decline and Fall of the Roman Empire CXXXVIII*

[11] Cheshire & North, *Private International Law* (11th Ed.) 1998 p. 16

[12] Cheshire & North, *op. cit.* pp. 16-17

municipal laws as well as commerce between one city and another gave rise to the need for recognition of alien laws and the beginning of rudiments of private international law.[13]

The glossators of the eleventh century did much to revive the Roman law. This was done by adding explanatory notes or glossary to the text of the *corpus juris.*

The local rules of cities like Bologna, Modena and Milan had become more or less independent from imperial rule and had developed in certain fields. Their legal provisions were in derogation from the common law of the Roman Western Empire and they also differed in content both in relation to the general law among themselves. This system, called *statuta,* came to symbolise, in a way, the growing independence of these new centres of power within the all-embracing framework of the authority of the Empire and they were recognised as locally valid. The consequence of this development of relationships affected citizens (domiciliaries) of different *communes* or property situated in another *commune,* or were executed in one town but had to be performed in another, or their enforcement was sought in a different country. The end result was the emergence of a complex legal web.[14] Such a situation could never be regarded as sound. Conflict rules had, therefore, to be found both as a matter of logic and practical utility. To clothe the law with an acceptable garment, resort was made to the Roman law. This therefore invested the rules with the same imperative and universal value with which the Roman law was noted.

The psychological need to establish a link between the rules required to supply an answer to the needs of the time and the superior legal wisdom (the *ratio scripta*) of the *juris corpus,* explains the curious historical fact that the medieval jurists were very eager to deal with the problem of *collisio statutorum* (conflict of statutes) in comments attached to passages of the Digest.[15] Wolff[16] has rightly opined that

---

[13] De Nova R. "Historical and Comparative Introduction to Conflict of Laws" (1966) *Recueil des cours* vol. 11 p. 443

[14] Ibid.

[15] It has been said that the comments had no relation whatsoever or at most had only an extremely attenuated relation to the digest. See for instance Niederer

though the Italian jurists broke entirely new ground, they pretended that they only developed rules latent in the *corpus juris*.

From these efforts grew a body of rules and principles that achieved an impressive statement by the mid-14th century in the work of Bartolus who taught in the universities of Bologna, Pisa and Perugia.

The statute theory was originated by the post-glossators. The object of which was to settle conflicts which arose not only between the local laws of the numerous Italian cities but also between the local laws that affected all the subjects of the Emperor of Germany and the king of Lombardy. Each statute was interpreted in order to ascertain its object and thus to fix its rightful sphere of application. In order to achieve this, each law was classified as relating to a person or a thing. A number of principles thus came into being. The principles could be seen from this classification:

> First, all statutes are either real, personal or mixed. A real statute is one whose principal object is to regulate things; a personal statute is one that chiefly concerns persons; while a mixed statute is one that concerns acts, such as the formation of a contract, rather than a person or thing.
>
> Secondly, these three categories of statute differ in their field of application. Real statutes are essentially territorial.
>
> Their application is restricted to the territory of the enacting sovereign. Personal statutes, on the other hand, apply only to persons domiciled within the territorial jurisdiction of the enacting sovereign, but they remain so applicable even within the jurisdiction of another territorial sovereign.

W, *Ceterum Quaero de Legum Imperii Romani conflictu* 49 Revue critique dedroit International Prive, Paris 1960, pp. 137-150 cited in Cheshire *op. cit.* p. 18

[16] Wolff M, *Private International Law* p. 26. An example of the method adopted could be seen from the gloss appended to the code of the Acursius as early as 1228. It went thus: "If a citizen of Bologna is sued at Modena, he ought not to be judged according to the statutes of Modena to which he is not subject, since it says (in the law *custos Populos quos nostrac clementias regit tempramentum*)".

> A personal statute of Florence overrides a Bologness personal statute if the Florentine does business in Bologna, provided that the business does not relate to statute. Mixed statutes apply to all acts done in the country of the enacting sovereign, even though they raise litigation in another country.[17]

Although this classification looks attractive, it proved to be inadequate in solving conflict of laws problems. First, it was difficult to determine in clear terms the statutes that were real and those that were personal. Secondly, issues that were outside that above classification had to be crammed into one of the recognised categories. Whatever may be said to criticise their effort, it is beyond doubt that the statutists set the fire of scientific discovery of private international law. This was the beginning of a functionally sound system of choice of law. By their approach, they conceived highly original methods to resolve multistate problems by making a principled selection among competing local rules.

Developments in some continental countries

The French School

Italian scholarship declined after Baldus, who outlived Bartolus by some 40 years.[18] The statute theory was carried into France and it was developed and refined by notable jurists like Dumoulin, D'Argentre and Gui Coquille. The existence of different provinces with separate systems of law called *coutume* or custom in France in the sixteenth century in France, like the thirteenth century Italy, paved the way for the development of conflict rules. Although the French kings had established the crown's supremacy, yet, the law varied from province to province. This was as a result of inter-provincial trade which were in constant conflict with each other.

---

[17] See Cheshire *op. cit.* p. 19
[18] See Juenger *op. cit.* p. 19

Dumoulin, a French scholar, like his Italian predecessors, attached his principal conflicts publication to the *lex cunctos populous*[19] much of which could be found in Bartolus commentary. His distinct contribution was in respect of his support of the party autonomy principle.[20] Although he could not be said to be the originator of this view, yet his emphasis of this notion at a time when conflicts scholars were pre-occupied with the classification of statutes, made his contribution noteworthy. He was of the view that all cases cannot be determined by the use of local laws. He felt that parties should be given the power to stipulate the law to govern their transaction in certain situations. He added that the principle of party autonomy should cover situations where the parties had failed to stipulate the applicable law. This idea of a "tacit agreement" or an "implied agreement" became the fore-runner of the modern idea of the "proper law" in the conflict of laws and the modern refinement of the "closest connection" or "most significant relationship" idea in the conflict of laws.[21]

D'Argentre was another major sixteenth century conflicts scholar. His idea was basically territorial. He derided the Italian school's "scholastic writers" and disagreed with the custom of attaching the conflict of laws to the *lex cunctos populos*. D'Argentre held the view, in a commentary on the coutume of Brittany, that conflicts rules are creatures of local, rather than universal law. He recognised only a limited number of personal laws. He brought in the category of "mixed statutes", which he contended should be treated like real ones.[22] He thus reduced the personal law idea to a mere exception. He emphasised the *lex rei sitae* and diminished the domiciliary law.

The significance of his approach lay in the fact that at the time he wrote, realty and disputes about marital property and succession to immovables were the main component of wealth and the bulk of legal

---

[19] See Gutzwiller M. Geschichte dea International Privatrechts at pp. 72-73, cited by Juenger in *Choice of law and Multistate Justice supra*.

[20] See Cheshire & North, *op. cit.* p. 20

[21] See generally Dicey & Moris *Conflict of Laws*: Morris, *Conflict of Laws*; Cheshire & North, *Private International Law*.

[22] See Juenger *op. cit.*

business. Such cases were generally adjudicated by the courts of the property's situs. His approach therefore favoured the use of the *lex fori*. D'Argentres approach was diametrically opposed to that of Dumoulin who emphasised the notion of a "tacit contract" and the application of a foreign law. The approach of D'Argentre' could be seen in the later works of Watcher and recent American authors.[23]

Guy de Coquille should also be mentioned. Unlike Dumoulin and D'Argentre, he wrote in the vernacular rather than in Latin. He distinguished between the Italian "statuta" and the French "Coutumes". He noted that whereas Italy had a shared *ius commune* which furnished the rule of decision, unless displaced by the statutum of one or the other city state, the French system lacked such a general law. By this is meant that he noted the essential difference between the legal environment in which Bartolus wrote and that of co-ordinate jurisdictions bereft of an over-reaching common law. In modern times, the approach of Guy de Coquille is relevant in the sense that conflict approaches developed in Federal systems, such as Nigeria or America whose component states share a common legal tradition may not work in Europe, where national codifications destroyed the unity that the reception of Roman law once provided.[24] De Coquille also adopted a purposeful approach to the issue of classification. Unlike his predecessors, he was of the view that the classification of laws as personal or real should not be based "on the mere shell of words, but on...the presumed and apparent purpose of those who have enacted the statute or custom.[25]

---

[23] See for example, Currie B. *Selected Essays on the Conflict of Laws* 183 (19630; Sedler, Interest Analysis and Forum Preference in the Conflict of Laws: A response to the "New Critics" 34 *Mercier L. Rev.* 593 (1983).

24 Iso Vitta. "The Impact in Europe of the American 'Conflicts Revolution'". (1982) *AM J. Comp. L.* I, 16 but see Juenger, "American and European Conflicts Law" 30 *Am. J. Comp. L.* 117 119 -130

[25] Juenger, *supra* p. 19

The Dutch authors

The seventeenth century Netherlands was a fertile ground for the development of conflict of laws. The Netherlands was organised as independent provinces but it had also become one of the major trading nations of the world. The extensive foreign commerce and political decentralisation engendered conflicts problems of national and supra-national dimensions.

Although the Netherlands was cosmopolitan in outlook, the doctrine of territorial sovereignty propagated by Bodin in the preceding century and elaborated by Grotius had taken root. There was therefore the need to make a strong case why a foreign law had to be applied in place of the local law. This resulted in the coinage of the phrase "conflict of laws" by the Dutch jurists. This gave the impression that choice-of-law problems are caused by the clash of sovereign commands. Unlike the Dutch jurists, the Italians did not bother about this notion because they believed that the Justinian code made it necessary to choose between the different *statute*. The French realised the inherent limitations of the reach of the forum's substantive rules and thus welcomed the application of foreign law.[26] Various approaches were adopted in this regard. Rodenbury, who was said to have coined the phrase "conflict of laws" tried to reconcile the application of foreign law with the idea of sovereignty by postulating a super-law derived from the "very nature and necessity" of the case, which bestowed extraterritorial effect upon local rules. Viewed critically, this explanation does not carry much weight for it does not explain in a scientific manner, the basis of the application of a foreign law in preference to a local law. Paul and Johannes Voet[27] used the notion of "comitas" as the basis for the application of a foreign law. This idea is traceable to the Justinian Digests.[28]

---

[26] Juenger, ibid.

[27] As Paul Voet's son, Johannes Voet explained that the notion of "comitas" reflects a principle noted in enlightened self-interest and convenience.

[28] Juenger, *op. cit.*

Huber also made comity the basis of his theory but unlike Robenburg and the Voets who were in favour of the framework of statutist tradition, Huber was against the classification of laws as personal, real and mixed. He based his idea of conflicts system on the two issues of sovereignty and comity. In the first chapter of his influential ten-page dissertation *"De conflict Legum Diversarum in Diversis Imperiis"*[29] entitled "Origin and use of the Question, Forensic Indeed, but belonging to the International rather than Civil Law; he said:

> the solution of the problem must be derived not exclusively from the civil law, but from convenience and the tacit consent of nations. Although the laws of one nation can have no force directly with another, yet nothing could be more inconvenient to commerce and to international usage than that transactions valid by the law of one place should be rendered of no effect elsewhere on account of difference in the law.[30]

Huber believed in the doctrine of comity as the basis for recognising foreign rules but he did not regard this as absolute. He maintained that a sovereign may refuse to recognise "rights acquired abroad if they would prejudice the forum's "power or rights". The contribution of Huber can be premised on five distinct heads, viz: (i) He heralded the demise of the statutist theory. (ii) He based recognition of foreign rules on international law. (iii) He emphasised the need for decisional harmony. (iv) He propagated the recognition of the vested rights doctrine. (v) He introduced the public policy reservation.

The above points are not without criticisms. First, it is difficult to reconcile the notion of sovereignty with the recognition of effects of multistate transactions. Secondly, the notion of comity as the basis for the recognition and enforcement of a foreign rule is not pungent enough as the forum state may decide not to recognise the law of a foreign state.

---

[29] Huberus U., Praelectiones Iuris Romani at Hodierni Pars 2, Lib 1, tit. 3 (1989), reprinted in Lorenzen E., *Selected Articles on the Conflict of Laws* 162-80 (1947) (with an English translation).

[30] Ibid. at p. 164-65

There can be no decisional harmony if each state reserves the right to disallow the application of a foreign law on the ground of public policy. As for the doctrine of vested rights, it could be said that it is difficult to determine whether a particular right has become vested before a decision is reached on it as rights are conclusions of law.

Despite the above criticisms, it is indisputable that the contribution of Huber has had an enduring effect on this subject. It has been opined of his essay:

> It is all printed in five quarto pages. In the whole history of law there are probably no five pages which have been so often quoted, and possibly so much read. They are distinguished by clearness, practical judgement and a total absence of pedantry.[31]

The above comment speaks a lot about the short but incisive book.

English private international law

The Norman conquest of 1066 led to the establishment of strong Kingship in England. The territorial and political organisation of England became centralised and the king's court became supreme over local tribunals. The royal courts possessed and exercised an original jurisdiction which was co-extensive with the realm and gradually evolved, out of a mass of local customs, common to the whole of the realm. This brought about the idea of a "common law" of England. Thus, by the twelfth century, the law that was administered by the courts had become the national "law of the land": Therefore unlike in Italy, France and the Netherlands, internal conflicts were unknown.[32] The necessary question which may be asked is: What became of Englishmen when they travelled outside England and entered into obligations or transacted business? Although they did travel but the common law did

---

[31] Harrison F., On Jurisprudence and the Conflict of Laws 116 (1919). Laine, *Introduction de Droit International prive* 104-105 (1888)

[32] Sack, *Conflict of Laws in the History of English Law: A Century of Progress 1835-1935.* Culp M. S. (ed.) *Selected Readings on Conflict of Laws* p. 3

not take cognisance of foreign cases. For example, as early as 1280, it was held that the common law courts had no jurisdiction to redress a tort committed abroad. In 1308, in the case of a writ of debt upon a document executed in Berwick in Scotland, it was said that "because it was made in Berwick, where the court has not cognisance, it was awarded that John took nothing by his writ."[33] This was the position till the seventeenth century.[34]

The reason for the failure of the English law to try cases having a foreign element could be deduced from the view of Reeves who said:

> by ancient constitution of the country in that respect still remaining unchanged, the whole administration of civil and criminal justice depended upon the jury system. [35]

Trial by jury was trial *per pais*, which meant (in the ancient language of the law), the country. A party was said to put himself upon the county. The jurors were local men cognisant, by their own knowledge, of the matter in dispute and were to be summoned upon the particular neighbourhood, vicinage (*vicinetum visne*) where the facts happened.[36] The pleadings were required to show the place (to lay the venue)[37] because, in executing the writ of *venire facias*, the Sheriff had to know from what neighbourhood the jurors would be summoned. It thus became the rule that a jury could not inquire into any matter that did not take place within the given locality.

---

[33] See *Hugh Le Pape* v *The Merchants of Florence* in London 8-9 Edw. 1 (1280-1281). Anonymous, Y.B.2 Edw. 11 (1308)

[34] Anonymous, Y. B. 2 Edw. 11 (1308)

[35] Reeves, *History of English Law* (Finlason's Ed. 1869) 301

[36] See Y. B., 48 Edw. III (1373) it was once held that "By the policy of our ancient law, the jury was to come *de vicineto*... and therefore they were summoned from the very hundred in which the cause of action arose" 2 *Hale H. C. L.* 135.

[37] Every allegation in the pleadings upon which issue could by taken i.e. every material and traversable allegation should state place at which the alleged fact happened. The old rules of venue were described in *Scott* v *Brest* 2 Term Rep. 238 (1788); *King* v *Burdett* 48 & Ald 175, 176 (1820).

This old rule suited England as it was in accordance with its social and economic regime which was land-holding, agriculture and other occupations of a local character.

By 1605, the developments that took place in respect of different kinds of personal property both in England and beyond the sea necessitated a modification of the ancient rule.

In order to remedy the anomaly of the old rule i.e. the withholding of relief in cases with foreign elements, English lawyers resorted to arid presumptions. For example, a tort committed in Paris, France was taken that the city was situated in England. Such a fiction had to be employed to make the matter triable by an English jury.

A judge deciding on an instrument dated in Hamburg, Germany said in 1625:

> We take it that Hamburg is in London in order to maintain the action which otherwise would be outside our jurisdiction. And while in truth we know the date to be at Hamburg beyond the sea, as judges we do not take notice that it is beyond the sea.

As late as 1774, a plaintiff could not have his suit tried in England unless he alleged that he had been falsely imprisoned on the Island of Minorca, "at London... in the parish of St. Mary le Bow, in the ward of cheap."[38] The defendant tried to object to this geographical incongruity but Lord Mansfield retorted that he "was embarrassed a great while to find out whether the counsel for the plaintiff really meant to make a question of it."[39] He stated further that what the law had done was to invent a fiction for the furtherance of Justice; and "...a fiction of law shall never be contradicted." It was therefore not necessary for the English courts to formulate choice of law rules.

The rules of trial at common law later began to undergo substantial changes.[40] The jury began to decide questions not only on account of his

---

[38] *Mostyn* v *Fabrigas* (1775) 98 E. R. 1021
[39] Ibid. at 1031
[40] Ibid. at 1030

own knowledge but also upon deposition of witnesses.[41] The initial step was to deal with "mixed cases." The other step, that of trying cases connected solely with a foreign country, was facilitated by the new division of actions into local and transitory.

It was not necessary to summon the jury from one particular neighbourhood in respect of transitory actions. The plaintiff could sue the defendant where he was found and could choose the venue he liked. By the time of Coke, it had been settled that the courts at Westminster could entertain all actions that were of transitory nature, such as actions for breach of contract or on bills of exchange, even if the relevant facts were connected with a foreign country. This was a radical departure from the old principle according to which the courts were administering their own law exclusively.[42]

The common law which was developed to meet the requirements of a feudal society proved inadequate in dealing with commercial and maritime cases. A solution which appeared to be in harmony with the old principles was found. Hitherto, commercial causes were determined by the law Merchant which was "the law of nations" and was administered in England and as such it was regarded as a law of England.[43] Thus, the English commercial courts applied a common

---

[41] Fortuescue, *De Laudebus Legum Angliae* (written soon after the year 1540. Ed. With notes by Selden, 2d Ed. Sworn in, & c., then either party, by himself or his counsel, shall open them all matters and evidence whereby he thinketh he may best inform them of the truth, and then either party may bring before them all such witnesses on his behalf as he may produce.... not unknown witnesses, but neighbours & C (C. 28): "The witnesses make their depositions in the presence of twelve creditable men, neighbours to the need that is in question, and to the circumstances of the same, and who also know the manners and conditions of the witnesses. and know whether they be men worthy to be credited or not".

[42] All restrictions in respect of venue have been removed by the Supreme Court of Judicature Act (1873).

[43] Coke once stated that "the law merchant is part of the laws of this Realm" and Lord Mansfield stated in *Luke* v *Lyde* (1759) 97 E. R. 614 at 617 "maritime law is not the law of a particular country, but the general law of nations. Blackstone was also of the opinion that "the affairs of commerce are regulated

European *lex mercatoria* and admiralty judges drew on sources widely scattered over time and space, such as the ancient sea law of Rhodes, the Consolat De Mar, the Roles d'Oleion and the laws of Wisby.[44] The common law courts however refused to apply this law as it was considered to be foreign.

The growth in English economic and financial relations with foreigners and the need for legal protection of such relations in England led to the establishment of the rule that foreign cases, at least as a general rule, should be left to be administered by foreign courts administering the foreign law applicable to such cases and that the English courts therefore, should, on proper occasions, give effect to foreign judgements in England. For example, Nottingham L. C. in *Cottington's case* once observed that:

> ...by the laws of England, for as we know not the laws of Savoy, so if we did, we have no power to judge by them; and *ergo*, it is against the law of nations not to give credit to judgement and sentences in foreign countries, till they be reversed by the law, and according to the form, of these countries where they are given.[45]

Thus, it became a firmly established rule in England that a foreign judgement creates a new cause of action in the nature of a simple contract,[46] suable in England as such debt and therefore without any condition of reciprocity.

The Treaty of Union of 1707 which preserved the Scottish legal system[47] facilitated the recognition of foreign laws. Scotland is a civil

---

by a law of their own, called the law Merchant or *Lex Mercatoria*, which all nations agree in and take notice of'. I W Blackstone, *Commentaries* 264.

[44] Juenger, *op. cit.* P.23. This comparative law tradition continued in England even after the common law judges encroached on the jurisdiction of the mercantile and admiralty courts, and early American admiralty cases also relied on foreign sources. See e.g. *Luke* v *Lyde* 97 E. R. 6 619; *De Lovio* v *Boit* (1815) 7 F. cas 418, 419 (C. C. D. Mass).

[45] 2 Swans 326 (1678).

[46] So held in *Dupleix* v *De Roven* 2 Vern 540

[47] See Anton A., *Private International Law* pp. 7-8 (2nd Ed. 1990)

law jurisdiction with institutions which differ from those of England. This gave rise to an early intra-British choice of law problems. Many Scottish jurists had studied on the Continent, especially in the Netherlands and were therefore familiar with the civil law system[48] and the civil and conflicts literature were usually cited in Scottish cases.[49]

The modern legal theory concerning conflict of laws was formulated in *Robinson* v *Bland*[50] in 1790. Lord Mansfield adopted the proposition stated by Huber that contracts are governed primarily by the law that the parties had contemplated. The question in this case was whether a contract which was valid by the law of France where it was made, though void by English law, could be sued upon in England. Lord Mansfield said:

> The general rule, established *ex comitate et jure gentium* is that the place where the contract is made, and not where the action is brought, is to be considered in expounding and enforcing the contract. But this rule admits of an exception when the parties at the time of making the contract had a view to a different kingdom.[51]

Thus by the eighteenth century, the seed of private international law had taken root. Although it could be said that many of the older decisions are faulty and could not guide us in the elucidation of rules for adjudication, yet it could be asserted that the eighteenth century marked the beginning of basic rules of private international law in England. Dicey, through his treatise, put in an orderly manner,[52] the position of private international law in England.

---

[48] Ibid. at p. 11

[49] See Nadelmann K. *Conflict of Laws: International and Interstate*

[50] (1760) 97 E. R. 717

[51] At p. 718

[52] One can see the influence of Huber and Holland in Dicey's treatise. For example, Dicey said: "To my friend and colleague professor Holland, also, I am under intellectual obligations of a special character. My whole conception of private international law has been influenced by views expressed by him, not only in his writings but in his conversation". A. Dicey, *A Digest of the law of England with Reference to the conflict of laws* vii (1896). He adopted the

The development of American conflict of laws

The federal nature of the United States of America made it a fertile ground for the development of private international law just like the Medieval Italy, pre- revolutionary France and the Dutch provinces during the Golden Age.

Prior to the American independence, the states, except Louisiana, adopted the English common law. After independence, the power accorded the constituent states to make laws and the judge-made laws further brought about divergence. This created choice of law problems.

The civilian legal literature was at first, treated with disdain. For example, Judge Porter in *Saul* v *His Creditors*[53] despite the profound comparative research which his judgement showed spoke of the research of Livermore on European scholarship in general as a "vast mass of learning" which left this "subject as much enveloped in obscurity and doubt, as it would have appeared to our own understanding."[54]

Samuel Livermore,[55] who lost the above mentioned case, put the research he did in respect of this case in a book form. In the book titled - Dissertations on the Questions which Arise from the Contrariety of the Positive Laws of Different states and Nations, he critisised Huber's

---

vested theory propounded by Huber and Holland. Dicey's General Principle No 1" reads: "Any right which has been duly acquired under the law of any civilised country is recognised and, in general, enforced by English courts, and no right which has not been duly acquired is enforced or, in general, recognised by English courts", Ibid. at xliii and 22; see also ibid. at 5 (citing Holland) 9, 10, 15, 23-32. It should also be stated that through Dicey, Huber's idea was adopted in the United States, where Joseph Beale, the editor of the First Restatement of conflict of laws made use of it as the basis for the rules of the Restatement.

[53] Juenger, Ibid. p. 27
[54] 5 Mart (N. S.) 569 (La 1827)
[55] See Juenger "Marital Property and the Conflict of Laws: A Tale of Two Countries" 81 *Col. L. Rev.* 1061. 1066-74, 1078-79 (1981).

comity doctrine and promoted the statutist learning.[56] Although not a popular book, it provided a valuable bibliography and compilation of civilian and common law sources in readily accessible form. This was effectively used by Story.

Story, an erudite Supreme Court Justice and Professor of law at Harvard shared Livermore's work and referred to civilian literature. Story painstakingly organised and analysed the rich continental literature as well as American, English and Scottish cases. His effort produced a massive and comprehensive work in systematic fashion. His judicial insights, common sense and awareness of the practical implications of conflicts rules and principles helped a great deal to produce this treatise.[57] The alternative title of this subject - private international law is usually attributed to him.

Story was opposed to the unilateralist approach of Livermore and the Statutist writers. He preferred Huber's axioms and the notion of comity. He was therefore in support of multilateralist approach. Of his commentaries it was said that he indiscriminately stung together excerpts from the works of foreign authors.[58] His treatise has been called one of the least scientific and one of the least conclusive books and lacking a "supreme guiding principle".[59]

On the other hand, Story's scholarly work had proved to be influential.[60] Indeed, it has been opined that, Bartolus Commentary excepted, no other work on the conflict of laws had proved to be as influential in Anglo-American literature, and except perhaps Huber's

---

[56] Concerning Livermore's background see de Nova, The First American Book on Conflict of Laws *8 Am. J. legal Hist.* 135 n. I. (1964).

[57] See De Nova ibid. p. 30

[58] Juenger, ibid. p. 30

[59] See Harrison *supra* at pp. 119-120. He said: "Heterogenous opinions based on a multitude of conflicting theories, drawn from writers extending over a period of five centuries, and of value utterly different, are tossed together almost like words in a dictionary".

[60] Ibid. at p. 119

essay.[61] Yntema, speaking of Story's commentaries maintained that it was "a pioneer comparative survey of both the civilian doctrines and the English and American precedents with a scholarly understanding that has not since been surpassed, and but barely equalled in England, the United States or indeed elsewhere.[62]

Beale, the editor of the first Restatement was not in favour of the notion of comity.[63] He also eschewed Story's reliance on foreign authorities.[64] He, like Dicey, put in place the vested rights doctrine.[65] The inadequacy of his approach led to its rejection and the adoption of the Second Restatement.

The German scholars

Carl Von Wachter an iconoclast and a legal positivist, in a German review debunked the views of the statutists, exposed the vested rights theory's circular reasoning and disparaged the doctrine of comity.[66] He

---

[61] See Von Bar, Theory and Praxis des International on Privatetrechts 65 (2nd ed. 1889) cited by Juenger Ibid. p. 30.

[62] Yntema, "The Historic Bases of Private International Law" (1953) 2 *A. M. J. Comp. L.* 297 at 307. He remarked that "At the time of their publication ... Story's Commentaries were without question the most remarkable and outstanding work on the conflict of laws which had appeared since the sixteenth century in any country and in any language". Savigny also paid tribute to Story and to Martin Wolff, Story was "the secret teacher of the world".

[63] See 3 Beale, *A Treatise on the conflict of Laws* x-x1

[64] I. Beale, *A Treatise on the Conflict of laws* x-x1 (1935)

[65] *Conflict of laws* x-x1 (1935)

[66] Nadelmann, Wachter's Essays on the "Collision of Private Laws of Different States" 13 *Am. J. Comp. L.* 414 (1963) (with translation of Wachter's "Guiding Principles" and Wachter's reply to Savigny's Criticism). In Wachter's words: "To claim absolute protection in the forum for a legal relationship created abroad according to foreign law is to argue from a premise that has not yet been established, and presupposes something that still needs to be proved, namely that the legal relationship is to be judged according to foreign rather than forum. For...the question whether someone

was in favour of the local law and he believed that a judge in determining issues must look "no doubt to the laws to which he is subject" i.e. the local law as he is an instrumentality ("organ") of the legislative will. The three "Guiding Principles" which Wachter recognised could be summarised thus:[67] That the courts must follow, first of all, any provisions of the lex fori that expressly designate the applicable law[68] absent such a directive, a judge faced with a conflicts problem should examine whether forum law must be applied in a given case notwithstanding the foreign element contained in the issue.[69] If on analysis, any doubt exists as to the applicable law, the judge should resolve it in favour of the *lex fori*.[70]

Unlike the forum-centered approach of Wachter, Friendrich Carl Von Savigny, whose conflicts classic was published in 1849[71] advocated an international approach to solving conflict problems. He made a decisive break with all former approaches. He dismissed the statute theory as being incomplete and ambiguous. He thus rejected the statistists' unilateralist approaches and the primacy of forum law advocated by Wachter. He envisaged the development of general principles of choice of law by legal science, that when perfected, would assure that the same result will be reached in all places. He was in favour of identifying all legal relationships for each and an appropriate

---

has acquired a right by virtue of an act done abroad depends, above all, on whether the act is to be judged by reference to foreign or to forum law."

[67] Juenger ibid. p. 32

[68] Watcher *supra* note 67.

[69] Watcher, ibid

[70] See Juenger, ibid. p. 33

[71] His conflicts classic was published as Volume eight of his system of current Roman Law. The volume contains two chapters. The first is devoted to the conflict of laws while the second is on intertemporal conflicts. Savigny was a theoretician. He preferred to rely on hypothetical cases rather than court reports to illustrate a point. This work was translated into English by William Guthrie in 1869. Discussions of Savigny's views could be seen in De Nova (1966) 11 *Hague Recueil* 454 - 464; Leipstein (1972) 1 *Hague Recueil* 131 - 135.

connecting factor that would tie it to a single legal system. An ideal rule to him is that which would be accepted by all states if proposed for inclusion in an international treaty, providing a "common statute law of all nations". The relevance of Savigny's approach lies in the fact that he suggested that each case should be decided according to the legal system to which it seems most naturally to belong.

The connecting factors, as they are now called, proposed by Savigny include.[72]

(a) Domicile for the resolution of issues like capacity, succession to estates and family relations.

(b) *Lex situs* for the determination of location of things.

(c) *Lex loci actus* for the determination of legal transactions like contract.

(d) *Lex fori* for the resolution of matters relating to procedure.

Although these choice of law rules had been in existence[73] since the time of Bartolus, they were organised by Savigny. He advanced a pragmatic consideration, rather than mere doctrinal musings in support of multilateralism.[74] His idea was cosmopolitan. in outlook and his contribution survived even till today as could be seen in the formulation of the "proper law" approach or the concepts of the "closest connection"

---

[72] See *Yntema,* ibid. at p. 310

[73] Livermore had earlier compared the nations of the civilised world to "one great society composed of many families between whom it is necessary to maintain peace and friendly intercourse *supra.* Grotius used the same thought to describe the essential unity of mankind. See Wise, Book Review 30 *Am J. Comp. L.* 362, 370. The Fiction of "voluntary submission of a person to a sovereign, on which Savigny relied can be traced to Huber and Grotius and his dislike of the vested rights theory and its description as "circular" is in line with Watcher's view. Watcher also used the question-begging "seat metaphor".

[74] Juenger ibid. p. 39

and the "most significant relationship"[75] Indeed, in the nineteenth century, some German courts allowed his views to prevail over statutory provisions[76] and in this century his teachings helped transform the unilateral conflicts provisions found in the original Introductory Act to the German Civil Code into a system of multilateral rules.[77]

Mancini

Mancini introduced the idea of the *Lex Patriae* when he gave his Inaugural address at the university of Turin entitled "Nationality as the Basis of International Law". He emphasised the fundamental importance of the ties of allegiance that link individuals to their home countries. His membership of a Parliamentary Commission that drafted the conflicts rules of the Introductory Provisions of the 1865 Italian code gave him the opportunity of transferring his postulates into the code.[78] He was of the view that all persons should be governed by the law of the state whose citizens they are. This was later identified as the national law. This principle was adopted by many in all central and Southern Europe as well as in Brazil, Japan and China and could be seen in the German, Swedish, Polish and many other legislations.[79] He also brought to the fore the *lex patriae* idea. He promoted as well the adoption of multilateral conflict treaties and participated in international projects pursuing that aim.[80] Although he attacked the doctrine of comity,[81] he defended the equality of forum and foreign laws.[82] He also considered

---

[75] See Dicey & Morris on the *Conflict of Laws* (12th Ed. 1993). Chaps. 10-13; see also the Rome Convention 1980 and see Restatement (Second) of Conflict of Laws, p. 145.

[76] See G. Kegel, *Internationales Privatrecht* 186-87, 183 (6th Ed. 1987); M. Wolff, *Internationales Privatrecht* 17 (1933) cited in Juenger ibid. p. 41.

[77] See A. Ehrenzweig *supra*

[78] Juenger ibid. p. 41

[79] See I. Rabel, *The Conflict of Laws* 121 -123 (2nd ed. 1958)

[80] See Nadelmann *supra* at 52-69, 69-71.

[81] Nadelmann *supra* at 52; see also de Nova *supra* at p. 466

[82] See Nadelmann, *supra* at p. 55

the role which public policy should play in the conflict of laws.[83] Indeed, he made enormous contribution to this subject.[84]

Nigeria

Prior to colonisation, there existed a number of local rules and customs by which Nigerians governed themselves. Apart from the local customs, the people, at least in the Northern part were in contact with citizens from other parts of Africa through the Trans-Savana trade. Rules were formulated, though in a rudimentary form, for the resolution of disputes between them. The coastal area of the South also came in contact with the European traders.[85]

The modern form of private international law in Nigeria is a by-product of the contact with the European countries. This was facilitated by colonisation.

With the arrival of the British, and the development of international trade and intercourse with several citizens of the world, the recognition and formulation of conflict rules became inevitable. The prevailing customary law systems which were basically unwritten could not cope with the municipal needs not to talk of international matters. With the acquisition of political power, the British introduced their legal system into Nigeria. New practices and institutions were thus introduced.[86]

In the determination of the history of private international law in Nigeria therefore, the first point of call is the common law-decisions of English law on private international matters, statutes of general

---

[83] See I. E. Vitta *supra* at p. 37

[84] Ibid. at 375-377. It should be pointed out that the discussion of Savigny on "strictly positive laws" failed to address the issue of public policy in a satisfactory manner.

[85] See generally, Webster J. B. and Boahen A. A: *The Growth of African Civilisation - The Revolutionary Years - West Africa since 180* Longman, 1967.

[86] For the sources and development of laws in Nigeria see Park W., *Sources of Nigerian Law*, Sweet & Maxwell (1963) (7th Ed.) ; See also Obilade A. O. *The Nigerian Legal System*, Sweet & Maxwell, 1st Ed. 1979

application - that is, the statutes that were in force in England on or before the 1st day of January 1900, in so far as those statutes are importable to Nigeria and have not been overridden by local statutes[87] and English statutes on specific matters.

Nigeria as an independent nation now has the power to make laws for herself.[88] The sources of private international law in Nigeria are Nigerian statutes, decisions of courts[89] and international obligations.[90]

---

[87] For the reception of English law in Nigeria, see S. 45 of the Interpretation Act cap. 89, 1958. See also the laws of various states except the former Western part of the country where the statutes of general application are not applicable. See also the Revised Edition of the Laws of the Federal Republic of Nigeria 1990. See generally Park W. Ibid.; Obilade A. O. ibid.

[88] See chapter 4 of the 1979 constitution

[89] See Park *op. cit.*

[90] See Park *op. cit.*

2

The objects and problems of harmonisation of private international law

The nature of trans-international transactions makes it imperative to apply the appropriate law in the determination of any issue having a foreign complexion. This idea is in accordance with the universal notion of justice and the need to promote the reasonable expectation of parties.

The legal order, however, is decentralised among a plurality of sovereign or autonomous authorities, asserting jurisdiction each within a defined territory over activities that concern their respective subjects.[1] Private International Law - a subject that has become the fugal music of law,[2] in an attempt to solve the problems created by plurality of laws, has brought to focus various approaches.

The initial notion of harmonisation, albeit rudimentary, is traceable to the Roman Empire. *Lus gentium* was the body of law initially developed by the *Praetor peregrinum* to resolve disputes between foreigners or between a foreigner and a Roman citizen. Even when the Italian and French scholars began to develop choice of law rules in the twelfth century, they still believed that the *ius commune* was a supra national law based, as it were, on Roman law. This could be regarded as the common law of the continental Europe.[3]

---

[1] See Chapter One for the discussion on the nature of private international law. See also Yntema H.E. "The Historic Bases of Private International Law" (1953) *Am.J. Comp.* L.297.

[2] Baty, *The Polarised Law* P.5

[3] Mcdougal L. III, "Private International Law: *Ius Gentium* versus Choice of Law Rules or Approaches" (1990) 38 *Am.J Comp. L.* 521. According to this writer, *ius gentium* which is now more known in public international law was

The idea of *ius commune* was however displaced in the nineteenth century by the idea of choice of law rules for the resolution of trans-jurisdictional problems.[4] This implies the application of the law of a particular country in a case having a foreign element without regard to the effect which that law may have. This approach does not enjoin the judge to consider the trans-national policies behind the choice of a particular law.

It should be pointed out that it is not in all cases that the application of a particular choice of law will direct the inquirer to an unambiguous solution. For instance, in trans-national tort cases, *lex loci delicti commissi* is the dominant choice of law rule.[5] Some states hold the view that this refers to the place where the wrongful act occurred.[6] Some prefer the place of injury.[7] In yet some nation states, the plaintiff or the court may select the law of the place of injury.[8] The meaning of *lex loci delicti* is not without controversy, this may refer to the place of the wrong or the place of injury. In yet some states, the *lex loci delicti* may not be applied at all. Reference may be to the law of the common domicile or habitual residence of the tortfeasor and the injured party.[9] This type of problem is not confined to tort cases, it could also be found

originally what is now commonly called "private" international law.
[4] Ibid.
[5] Generally Morse C.G.J., "Choice of Law in Tort: A Comparative Survey" (1984)32 *Am.J. Comp. L.*51
[6] See for example The Austrian Law of June 15, 1978 translated in Palmer, "The Austrian Codification of Conflicts Law" (1980)28 *Am.J. comp. L.* 445.
[7] Restatement (first) of Conflict of Laws s.377 (1934).
[8] Such countries include China. See Chen, "Private International Law of the People's Republic of China: An Overview (1987) 35 *Am. J. Comp. L.* 445 at 469; Hungary See Gabor, "A Socialist Approach to Codification of Private International Law in Hungary: Comments and Translation (1980) 55 *Tul. L. Rev.* 63 at 81 See generally Morse *op. cit.*
[9] Such nation states include Austria, See Palmer *supra* n. 6 at 220; East Germany, See Juenger, "The Conflicts Statute of the German Democratic Republic: An Introduction and Translation" (1977)25 *Am.J. Comp. L.* 332 at 348. See Morse, *supra* at 61.

in contract and succession.

The effect of this confusion is lack of uniformity in respect of the facultative elements to be employed in the resolution of conflict problems. The viable alternative is to harmonise the basic principles of private international law. Certain benefits enure from this approach. The benefits could be seen from the following discussion.

Harmonisation brings about practical predictable rules for the determination of the appropriate law to apply in solving practical problems on uniform basis. For example, the choice of law rules of various nations relating to succession had reached a crisis proportion before the harmonisation effort of the Hague Conference on the law applicable to the estates of deceased persons.[10] The established rules under the Anglo-American common law differed from those of the civil law. It cannot be doubted that almost all nations have succession rules and most of them provide for succession to about the same members of the decedent's family, but the variations in the size of indefeasible shares or interest shares of spouses and other family members make choice of the applicable law crucial.[11] Furthermore, the distinction between the rules applicable to movables and immovables by the traditional Anglo-American legal system has become obsolete given modern property interests. This doctrine, known to the common lawyer as the doctrine of scission is alien to a civil lawyer. This dichotomy has given rise to complex litigation in the common law world.

Harmonisation enhances the inter-play of legal collaboration and mutual respect between various legal systems. The various legal systems differ in structure and allocation rules. The use of various choice of law rules as a means of solving conflict problems has proved to be inappropriate necessitating further and better co-operation. This need calls for the abandonment of some rules which are unsuitable for international co-operation. This of course does not mean that nations are giving up their sovereignty, but it is a step in search for certainty in the

---

[10] See Scoles E.F., "The Hague Convention on Succession" (1994) *Am. J. Comp. L.* 85.

[11]. Scoles E.F. *supra* pp. 86-87.

law, protection of reasonable expectation of parties and promotion of international commerce and co-existence. The EEC legal order established pursuant to Article 220 of the EEC Treaty is an example in this regard. One essential feature of this legal order is the convergence of various legal systems. The EEC, which was initially a community of six,[12] now has more than twelve member states with over nine languages and at least thirteen legal systems, some of which are very different from each other. Despite this scenario, the EEC is an example of success in trans-national co-operation. Specifically, the EEC Convention on Jurisdiction and Enforcement of Foreign Judgements, otherwise called the "Brussels Convention" has proved that there is much to be gained in legal co-operation. The exorbitant rules of jurisdiction have become history in the member states. In the language of Article 2:

> subject to the provisions of this Convention, persons domiciled in a contracting state shall whatever their nationality, be sued in the courts of that state. Persons who are not nationals of the state in which they are domiciled shall be governed by the rules of jurisdiction applicable to nationals of that state.

From this singular effort, the following advantages are derivable:
(i)   It has put an end to divergent requirements for the recognition and enforcement of judgements obtained from another country, but

---

[12] The European Economic Community was made up of six member States at inception in 1957. They were Belgium, France, the Federal Republic of Germany, Italy, Luxembourg and the Netherlands. The Treaty establishing this community (otherwise called the Treaty of Rome) was adopted in March 1957 (March 25, 1957) and it entered into force on January 1, 1958). In 1973, the Community gained three additional Member States upon the accession of the United Kingdom, Ireland and Denmark. Greece became the tenth Member State in 1981. The Accession of Spain and Portugal brought the total number of member states to twelve. Some other Eastern European countries like Sweden and Finland had voted to join the European Community. Norway however voted against joining.

which is a party to the Convention.[13]

(ii) There now exists uniform connecting factor for the assumption of jurisdiction by courts of the member states.[14]

(iii) Parties still retain the power under Article 17 to choose a particular law which is of interest to them.[15]

(iv) There is a uniform final appellate court for the interpretation of the rules of the Convention and for determining disputes.[16]

(v) Convergence of various legal traditions and enrichment of common European legal system.

(vi) Encouragement of co-operation among the member states.

(vii) Prohibition of the application of that slippery concept - public policy, in the determination of the validity of the judgment obtained from the court of a contracting state.[17]

(viii) Development of autonomous jurisprudence through a cosmopolitan approach to the interpretation of principles and concepts.[18]

(ix) Prohibition, or at least, reduction of the problem of litigation about where to litigate.[19]

(x) Reduction of the problem of lawyers in advising clients on the position of the law thereby bringing about reasonable

---

[13] It should be pointed out that hitherto, there was no uniformity in respect of the requirements of the law in granting recognition to judgments obtained from foreign jurisdictions. For example, France required that the matter be tried all over again. It may however be said that some requirements are common to most jurisdictions. Such requirements include observance of the rule of fair hearing, finality of judgment, absence of fraud and possession of jurisdiction.

For example under the common law, service of the writ is the requirement for assumption of jurisdiction. The community law talks of domicile.

[15] See Morse C.G.J. *op. cit.*

[16] This is the European Court of Justice at Luxembourg.

[17] See Article 28 of the Brussels Convention.

[18] See for example *L.T.U.* v *Eurocontrol* case 29/76.

[19] See generally Morse C.G.J. "Litigation about Where to Litigate", text of a Paper - delivered by Prof. C.G.J. Morse in London in 1995.

predictability of result.[20]

Despite harmonisation, opportunity to make reservations ensures that negotiations need not become deadlocked indefinitely through the intransigence of parties whose legal traditions and institutions appear too difficult to reconcile with those of the members of any consensus which may be emerging.[21] Thus, if a particular country feels strongly about an issue, instead of opting out of the legal co-operation, it may decide to make reservations in respect of certain areas of the Convention.[22]

Harmonisation encourages co-operation and systemisation of rules of law of various states. The Hague Convention on succession is an example in this regard.

Where a jungle of rules exists, it would be impossible to give safe advice to clients. Harmonisation avoids the costly, confusing and delay which are necessary incidents of divergent choice of law rules. There is nothing as discouraging like having to enter a caveat when a lawyer has to give a professional advice as to the state of the law. The consequence is that mobility will be hampered because the foreign law may not only be difficult to understand, it may also be patently difficult to ascertain. A trader will therefore need to study and take into consideration the law of the foreign country he proposes to visit. This would be more difficult if the official language is foreign to him. The businessman, as noted by Lando,[23] will therefore often feel the same frustration as did Voltaire, when he travelled to France, where the laws changed everywhere he

---

[20] For a full discussion of the Convention, See L. Collins, T. Hartley, J. McClean & C. Morse, Dicey & Morris on the Conflict of Laws (12th Ed.) 1993 & Supp. 1994 Chaps. 11-14, Cheshire & North's *Private International Law* (12th Ed. 1992) Chaps. 14 & 16; A Dashwood, R. Hacon & R. White *Guide to the Civil Jurisdiction and Judgments Convention* (1987).

[21] See Fletcher, *Conflict of Laws and European Community Law* (1982) p.7.

[22] For example, Article 22 of the Rome Convention allows any contracting state, at the time of signature, ratification, acceptance or approval to reserve the right not to apply a provision of the Treaty.

[23] Lando O, "Principles of European Contract Law: An Alternative to or A Precursor of European Legislation" (1992) 40 *Am. J Comp. L.* 573 at 575.

changed horses.

Furthermore, harmonisation brings about cross fertilisation of ideas and enriches community laws. This is because some principles of law which could be elevated to the international level but which are confined to a particular jurisdiction may be made use of when nation states come together to make communal laws. For example, the European court of Justice was established pursuant to the 1971 protocol to the Brussels Convention. Judges of this court are from various legal regimes. Each country has contributed one thing or the other to the system of justice in this court. The European court of justice shows traces of habits acquired in the context of national legal systems.[24] The French legal system has bought, among other things, its impersonal style of writing judgments without any dissent or minority opinion; the advisory opinion of one member of the court - the advocate general and the deductive style of reasoning i.e. inference of rules from broad maxims and solutions to legal problems from those rules preferably by a chain of logically correct deductions. The Dutch and German influence could be seen from the adoption of a flexible approach to the determination of legal issues rather than logical deductions; the principle of proportionality, which, as interpreted by a British member of the court, means that you do not crack a nut with a sledge-hammer. This means that the court must consider the proportionality or relevance of a rule to a particular issue. The German Federal system from which emerged its federal constitutional court had developed concepts on relations between federal and state power which has been transposed to relations between community institutions and national authorities. Furthermore, this contact has made possible constant review of community legislation and the idea of declaring invalid national laws which are incompatible with community law. Over the years, the court's way of reasoning became less deductive and podictic.[25]

---

[24] For the contribution of various legal systems, See Koopmans T., "The Birth of European Law at the Crossroads of Legal Traditions (1991) 39 *Am. J. Comp. L.* 493 at 499-500.

[25] Koopmans T. *Op. cit.*

The common law made its way to the community by the Accession of the United Kingdom, Ireland and Denmark. The idea of precedent was introduced as well as the inductive way of reasoning - that is, the idea of climbing from the facts to the rules to be applied, rather than deducing rules from more general rules. The community has also gained the Anglo-American system of delivering an individual opinion, which system allows him to speak his mind. The community court has also benefitted from the important role assigned to procedure in the determination of disputes.[26]

Another important contribution of the common law is the development of a system of exchange of information and opinion between the bar and the bench. By this system, questions are put to the parties' agents or counsel, either in writing or orally at the hearing. This creates an atmosphere conducive to dialogue between the bench and the bar, during which the main issues will be identified and attention will be concentrated on the essential arguments concerning these issues. The dialogue will thus contribute to a better understanding of the case, especially by the advocate general and the judges. By reason of the intellectual strength of its comparative methods, the community's judicial institution has become one of the major sources of legal innovation in Europe.[27] National courts take heed of the court's way of reasoning thereby creating a contra-flow of ideas.[28]

Harmonisation encourages globalisation of private business. Rules of law become uniform and predictable and international trade is better served and developed. Since this is the desiratum of private international law, the advantage in this respect cannot be over-emphasized. Indeed, national boundaries are, by and large, irrelevant to men of commerce, since the place of the assets of a merchant may be more important to him than his accidental place of birth.

The economic advantage of harmonisation should also be emphasised. Economically, judicial judgments would enjoy full freedom

---

[26] Koopmans T., *Op. cit.*

[27] Koopmans T., *Op. cit.*

[28] See generally Koopmans Ibid.

of circulation as goods, persons, services and capital. This could be vividly seen from the EEC community arrangement. For example, Dr. H.C. Ficker, speaking in the context of the harmonisation of the company laws of the Member states stated:[29]

> Differences in the Member States' legislative and administrative provisions affect the establishment or functioning of the common market. They hamper the free circulation of goods, persons and capital, provoke distortion in competition making unequal the burdens on the competing national industries and are, therefore, obstacles for the development of the common market to the same extent as the maintenance of tariff borders or of different national policies in the various economic fields. Therefore, these differences have to be abolished.

This conclusion is also relevant in other areas of Private International Law. In a note sent to the member states on October 22, 1959 inviting them to commence negotiations as envisaged in Article 220 of the founding Treaty, the commission of the European Economic Community stated: [30]

> a true internal market between the six states will be achieved only if adequate legal protection can be secured. The economic life of the community may be subject to disturbances and difficulties unless it is possible, where necessary by judicial means, to ensure the recognition and enforcement of the various rights arising from the existence of a multiplicity of legal relationships. As jurisdiction in both civil and commercial matters is derived from the sovereignty of Member States, and since the effect of judicial acts is confined to each national territory, legal protection and, hence, legal certainty in the common market are essentially dependent on the adoption by

---

[29] Fletcher, *op. cit.*

[30] Morse C.G.J. *International Shoe* v *Brussels and Lugano*: Principles and Pitfalls in the Law of Personal Jurisdiction" text of a paper delivered at a conference held at the University of California, February 1995. This was also cited in the Official Report on the original Brussels Convention of 1968 by P. Jenard O.J. 1979 C 59/1,3.

Member States of a satisfactory solution to the problems of the recognition and enforcement of judgements.

The above, which could be regarded as a tip of the iceberg highlights the multifarious advantages of harmonisation of private international law.

Despite the advantages inherent in the idea of harmonisation, there are also some disadvantages which harmonisation may produce. The disadvantages include the following:

Harmonisation entails the convergence of various legal systems. A necessary consequence of this is that nations without common political, economic social interest, outlook or tradition will come together and formulate common rules for the resolution of problems of international dimension. It is beyond doubt that when a nation feels strongly about an issue which the uniform law regulates, it will stultify that law by resorting to some escape devices for the purpose of not giving effect to the uniform laws. This may therefore negate the essence of harmonisation.

At the level of concluding multilateral Conventions, the final agreement is usually an end product of unbridgeable abyss[31] which separates different national or sometimes regional traditions. As Fletcher rightly pointed out,[32] even where a consensus can be achieved among a majority of the participants, the probability remains that several of the states whose representatives helped formulate some hard-fought compromise will deem it fit to refrain from actually becoming parties to the Convention which embodies it, whilst those states for whom even the original compromise was unacceptable will, *afortiori*, be disinclined to accede to the Convention.

What is more, even when a Convention is acceded to, it may be subject to reservations and denunciation which makes it less attractive as a vehicle of legal integration. Reservations distort the framework of a Convention. The hard negotiations among the Member States may

---

[31] Fletcher, *Op. cit.* P.6.
[32] Fletcher, Ibid.

become a nullity where a nation is permitted to contract out of a Convention.

Like any other instrument of international law making process, a Convention must be negotiated, signed and ratified by the participating states for it to be effective. This usually takes time. If the Convention is ultimately adopted, several years may have passed between the period of negotiation and ratification.

Harmonisation efforts may be stultified by conservative and nationalistic attitude usually adopted by lawyers for whom their national law is the best.

Harmonisation involves the participation of many countries with diverse culture and language. For example, the European Economic Community is made up of not less than 13 legal systems and nine languages. The Convention therefore "speaks in many tongues".[33] The four original languages of the Convention as represented by the four authentic texts were Dutch, French, German and Italian. Following the accession of Britain, Ireland and Denmark, English, Irish and Danish were added. Greek, Spanish and Portuguese have also been added. As some of the Lugano states have indicated to join the EEC, their languages will also be recognised. Thus terms which were originally conceived by the community of six must be translated to the additional languages even if no identical terms can be found in those languages. Mutilation of terms in the course of such transformation cannot be ruled out.

A consequence of entering into a Convention may be the inhibition of necessary law reform. If a state is bound by an international obligation to adopt a rule it cannot subsequently enact another rule instead even if it has become abundantly clear that the rule agreed upon is working injustice and that other rule is much to be preferred. The consequence is that the possibility of legal experimentation is reduced.

Allied to a point noted above is that which concerns the drafting of Conventions in one principal language which language is the only authentic text e.g. the French version of the Warsaw Convention on

---

[33] Morse *op. cit.* p.14

Carriage by Air is the authentic version. The English legislation implementing the Convention contains both the French text and the English translation, and provides that if there is inconsistency the French prevails. Even where one or more versions are all authentic, one faces the problem of the texts not matching one another.

Where harmonisation is regionally based, this type of grouping does not always take into consideration the incidents of their regional laws on states that are not members of the group. For example, the EEC Convention displays a propensity to work in a sinister way towards those that are not resident somewhere within the borders of the community. The Convention permits the utilisation of the rules of exorbitant jurisdiction against non-residents in the contracting states. It therefore means that justice is a double-barrel instrument. While some rules are for members of the community, others are for those outside it. It is doubtful if the desire to have global co-operation can be served by the adoption of this method.

Co-operation brought about by harmonisation may not necessarily promote uniformity especially if various national courts have to interprete rules of a Convention the way they deem fit. National courts do not possess requisite legal environment for the development of uniform rules. It is probable that national courts will always resort to home made laws.

The problems highlighted above are general. There are however some problems which are peculiar to developing countries. Problems of harmonisation of Private International Law in the developing countries will thus be considered separately.

Problems of harmonisation of private international law in the developing countries.

It is in the developing countries that the problem of harmonisation is more acute. African nations have just emerged into independent entities. It is not out of place to argue that given the time frame of their existence, there is no pressure to bring their laws together by way of harmonisation. It could even be said that given the multifarious internal and international problems that developing countries face, harmonisation of laws would be one of the least priorities of such nations. The above issues highlight the way some African nations view harmonisation. Other reasons include the following.

Most developing countries view harmonisation of laws as an infringement on their sovereignty. This is a chauvinistic view. This is because harmonisation does not disturb the sovereignty of a nation. It is rather a step in the right direction since harmonisation brings about reasonable predictability of laws and may work as an instrument of economic development. The issue of sovereignty is indeed irrelevant in this respect.

Harmonisation is also hampered by problems such as lack of adequate legal education, access to basic research materials and legal scholarship. Sound legal education is a necessary condition for harmonisation as the law of more than one state will have to be considered. If sufficient experts cannot be found harmonisation will be a mirage. Allied to this is the requirement of availability of basic research materials. Furthermore, the interpretation of the rules is a necessary task for the judges. This calls for legal scholarship and availability of trained or experienced judges who can take up complex legal issues. It is disheartening to note that some countries still rely on judges from other countries to beef up their judiciary.[34]

It must also be pointed out that unnecessary suspicion among developing countries hampers harmonisation. For example, in the West African sub-region, lack of trust between the English speaking and French speaking nations has affected sub-regional co-operation and development.

Political instability and spiral economic problems which developing countries have to contend with make harmonisation a less-pressing issue. For example, it will be difficult to bring Somalia or Liberia to attend any conference on a Convention to harmonise rules of private

---

[34] For example, Nigeria sent some of her legal personnel to Uganda and Botswana some years ago. There are also some Nigerian Judges currently serving in Gambia.

international law. These are nations, among others, facing the problem of national survival. Harmonisation is therefore not a priority for a nation that is at war or one facing acute economic problems.

Lack of information as regards the legal systems of other developing nations is another problem militating against harmonisation of laws. Garro,[35] stating the position in respect of the Latin American States observed that it may be surprising to foreign observers to realise how little informed Latin American lawyers are about the legal systems of their sister Republics. He added that Latin American Law Revision Commissions, judges, law professors and lawyers communicate with each other very little, but most often in conferences that take place in Europe or the United States. The most sophisticated legal comparativists, he said, are likely to be more acquainted with some aspects of the law of commercial transactions in France, Spain, Italy or even Germany or New York than with the legal system of another Latin American country.[36]

Where adequate resources are available, it is doubtful if a

---

[35] Garro A.M. "Unification and Harmonisation of Private Law in Latin America" (1992) 40 *Am. J.C.L.* 587 at 610-611.

[36] A feature of the Latin American legal systems is that they share a similar socio-economic structure, political culture and a common legal heritage. The idea of harmonisation is not new to nations of Latin America. In the nineteenth century, the idea of unification was shown in the adoption of comprehensive multilateral treaties on private international law. In actual fact, Latin America made the first attempt in the world to codify rules on private international law at a time when lawyers and governments in Europe were beginning to see the advantages inherent in this method. Thus, in 1875 the Peruvian government convoked a group of Latin American jurists to Lima with the aim of determining whether the Latin American community had sufficient concordant conceptions to agree on uniform codes of private law. The congress of Lima however gave up the idea of drawing up uniform codes of substantive law as it was felt that efforts to even out national rules on the conflict of laws and co-ordinate policies on inter-American litigation was more Garro A.M. "Unification and Harmonisation of Private Law in Latin America (1992) 40 *Am. J.C.L.* 587 at 610-611.

notoriously under paid academic community and an understaffed and overworked judiciary would be able to process, digest and think over the many intricate issues posed by legal harmonisation. This is because the above factors naturally affect the productivity or the output of the personnel that bring about practical solution to human problems at the international level.

Also, most of the developing countries are not members of international bodies for the harmonisation of laws. Many believe that these international bodies merely protect the interests of developed nations and as such inappropriate as viable vehicles of legal integration. For example, a handful of West African and Latin American countries are not members of the Hague Conference or the Unidroit.

Divergence in the political, economic, social and cultural background of various nations is also a militating factor for non-grouping by some of the developing countries.

Developing countries are not free from manipulation by their former colonial masters. The consequence of this is that most developing nations hardly maintain a position different from that of their former political masters. This should ordinarily not be a problem if it is done in the interest of their nations but most African leaders do this to perpetuate themselves in power.

The unarticulated distrust that international instruments favoured the interests of industrialised nations at the expense of developing countries is another problem militating against harmonisation.

Allot[37] also put some of the problems in this respect in focus when he noted that African nations face several problems such as (i) maintenance of constitutionality and the very existence of the nation against military and personal ambitions of divisive tribal leaders (ii) overcoming the disadvantages left behind by the colonial carving up of Africa in the way of lines of communication which go to the wrong direction and of linguistic and administrative barriers that reinforce political frontiers; (iii) procuring a speedy growth in the national product

---

[37] Allot A., "The Unification of Laws in Africa" (1968).

and a consequent off-take in the form of schools, medical facilities, and all the other desirable features of a welfare society, and (iv) eliminating pockets of social injustice based on racial, ethnic, sex or religious differences. Given the above, one can conclude that it is necessary to eliminate the barriers.

On a general note, it could be said that while the idea of harmonisation is very significant , problems beset this idea and unless these problems are eliminated or reduced it would be difficult for nation states to come together for the purpose of bridging the legal gap that separates them or that pose a serious threat to supra-national trade, co-existence and co-operation.

3

Institutions or bodies involved in the harmonisation process outside Africa

Effective harmonisation process cannot take place unless there are organised bodies involved in this process. The basic idea behind this process is functional international legal co-operation. The above assertion, without more, does not or should not confine this process to efforts by nation states since the aim of private international law is not merely to prevent conflicts between states but also to provide effective mechanism for obviating hardship to individuals, hence the need to consider efforts by supra-national bodies. This basic idea was put in focus by Professor Asser who said:

> The most dangerous of conflicts law is without any doubt that between laws relating to the conflict of laws, because such a conflict occasions the certainty of uncertainty.[1]

This discussion will be considered from two dimensions. They are efforts by international bodies and regional organisations outside Africa. The former include
  i. The Hague Conference on Private International Law;
  ii. The Unidroit and
  iii. The Uncitral.

In respect of the latter, the efforts of
  i. The European Economic Community; and

---

[1] This remark was made by Professor Asser, one of the founders of the conference at the fourth of the Hague Conferences. Cited by **Anton** *Private International Law* (2nd ed.) p.45., T.M.C. Asser presided over the first 4 sessions of the Conference (1893, 1894, 1900 and 1904).

ii. The Council of Europe; will be considered.

However, before this discussion is undertaken, it needs to be emphasised that our world is divided among plurality of states, each asserting authority and imposing its own legal system within the confines of the geographical boundaries that constitute each as a nation, but no nation is an island hence the need for co-operation.[2]

This need for intercourse brings to focus the usefulness or the necessity to have viable institutions whose primary aim is the harmonisation or unification of laws. This need was clearly stated by Molengraff when he wrote:

> The increasing international intercourse, the increasing community of interests have gradually led to the realisation that human race does not consist of a collection of as many separate and individual societies of legal communities as there are states, but that it constitutes one society, one legal community-not-withstanding the fact that legislation and administration of justice are locally different and that the world has been divided into states, just as each state has been divided into provinces and districts, for the purpose of orderly administration. The society of mankind constitutes one body that has commissioned the care of certain interests to a number of governments, each operating within an assigned territory. This consciousness is continuously growing and expressing itself in various ways in the field of the law. It is on account of this growing consciousness of the unity of the human race that a world law is coming into being, also in the field of civil law.[3]

He also noted the obstacles inherent in this idea. As he pointed out:

> A great number of obstacles and legislative nature obstruct the

---

[2] Baty, *The Polarised Law* P.5

[3] W.P.L.A. Molengraff, *De dageraad Van het Wereldrecht* pp. 89 - 113 cited in G. J. W. Steenhoff, *Dutch Attitude Concerning the Unification of Private International Law* p.223.

way; nationalism and the principle of sovereignty, the notion of independence as well as the diversity of conceptions regarding the law constitute dividing forces that oppose the urge to co-operate, and act as a drag towards the consciousness that all states are part of one world society and are called upon to jointly maintain the legal order within that society.[4]

Despite the obstacles, the importance of harmonisation cannot be over-emphasised and *afortiori*, the harmonisation institutions are of vital importance in private international law.

The Hague conference on private international law

This institution was the first fruit of co-operation between almost all the European States in their effort to harmonise or unify private international law. This idea contained, according to Molengraff;

A promise for the future, it opens a new era in the history of the law, an era wherein after the present dawn the day of world law may be expected.[5]

The aim of the Hague Conference on private international law was and still is to work towards international unification of the rules of conflict of laws. The activities of the Hague Conference in its over one hundred years of its existence have, in the main, been devoted to producing Conventions unifying the rules of private international law.

The Hague Conference on Private International Law may be described simply as an inter-governmental international organisation that drafts Conventions (or treaties) in the field of Private International Law. It is sponsored by the Dutch government and meets in the Hague in plenary session, usually every four years. As at March 1990, about 36 states were members. The aim of this organisation is to seek to achieve the harmonisation of rules of private international law in the member

---

[4] Ibid. p. 224
[5] Molengraff, Ibid., Steenhoff Ibid.

states. This is in line with Article 1 of the Statute of the Hague Conference which states:

> La Conference de la Haye a pour but de travailler a l'unification progressive des regles de droit international prive.[6]

Prior to the establishment of the Hague Conference, Mancini's idea of a universal or supranational system of private international law held away. Although he stressed the importance of nationality, but apparently paradoxically, Mancini and his disciples were internationalists in outlook. They pressed the European governments to convene an international conference for the purpose of securing the law.[7]

The first International Conference on Private International Law was held at the Hague in 1893. The aim was to reach a common accord in matters of private international law by way of international Conventions. The 1893 conference was attended by most of the mainland European states including Russia, Austro-Hungary and Denmark. Japan became a member in 1904. It took time before the United Kingdom joined the Hague Conference. It did not join until 1925 apparently because the Conference sought to apply the principle of nationality as the key to every legal problem.[8]

It has been suggested that the success of the conference at the beginning if its proceedings was due to its very uniformity of outlook. Conventions were prepared on diverse issues. There were Conventions on Marriage, Divorce, Guardianship of Minors, Interdiction, the effects of Marriage on Property and Civil procedure.[9] For example, the Convention on Civil procedure was adhered to by 23 States. It provided for the services of documents, letters rogatory and similar issues abroad. It was later replaced in 1954.

The work of the Conference was disrupted by the first world war. A fifth session was however convened in 1925. Britain attended the 1955

---

[6] Anton Ibid.
[7] Anton Ibid.
[8] Anton Ibid.
[9] Anton Ibid.

Conference for the first time. The success of the past, made the conference to contemplate works on Bankruptcy, Succession, the Enforcement of Foreign Judgements and International Sales of Goods. The draft Conventions were however not signed by the states.

The sixth session was in 1928. After this session, the Conference put a hold on its activities as a result of the international tensions of the 1930's and ultimately, the World War II.

The Seventh Conference took place in November 1951, after the Second World War, on the initiative of the Council of Europe. More states were admitted during this Conference. The states included Ireland, Greece, Turkey and Iceland. The Seventh Conference established the statute or Constitution of the Conference which formally entered into force on July 15, 1995 during the eighth Conference. The Convention on International Sales of Goods was also produced at this Conference. The Hague Conference has been meeting regularly from then and has initiated many Conventions on private international law. Indeed, it has become a strong pillar in the harmonisation of private international law rules.

Organisation and process of harmonisation by the Hague conference

The general plan is that the conference meets in plenary session every four years. Its agenda is determined by suggestions made by Member States. The suggestions are considered by a body called the Commission d'Etat Neelandaise (Netherlands State Commission), a purely Dutch organ. Despite the nationalistic outlook of this organ, it carries on its work in an international spirit. It considers suggestions put to it but it reserves to itself the discretion to determine the ultimate agenda to be used. It also determines the timing of the sessions. In 1951, the Conference established a Permanent Bureau to ease its task and to perform other preparatory work for the future meetings of the conference. The Bureau is directed by a Secretary General. The establishment of the Bureau facilitated the secretarial services at the conference. Furthermore, the joining of the common law countries, made it necessary to adopt a new attitude to the task of unifying private international law. For example, the deductive method of the earlier conference had to be dropped for new methods based upon a close study of the actual rules in force in different legal systems.

The Hague Conference has grown from an association of isolated states brought together by the Netherlands Government to become an international organisation meeting in plenary session in principle every four years with representatives of states from all parts of the world.

New states may join on the proposal of an existing member of the conference. The proposal must be accepted by a majority[10] of the Member States that vote on the question. As the Conference is presently constituted, majority of the Member States are from the Western Europe.

Structurally, the working methods of the Hague Conference involve a collaborative effort between, on the one hand, the permanent Bureau and the Commission d'Etat Neerlandaise, and on the other hand, between the Permanent Bureau and the Foreign Offices and Ministries of Justice of Member States in respect of matters of finance and overall policy.

A representative explanation of the process of harmonisation of law by the Hague Conference is as follows:

> A Member State of the conference puts forward a suggestion regarding a topic on which harmonisation is **desirable**. Arguments would be made in support of the topic. This suggestion will normally be considered by one of the Commissions of the conference charged with making recommendations about its future work. The Commission is to decide whether or not to recommend the retention of the suggested topic. If its retention is recommended, it will then be submitted to the Netherlands State Commission. This being the body that has the overall responsibility through a Permanent Bureau of the organisation of the Hague Conference.

If the recommendation for the retention of the topic is accepted by

---

[10] Anton Ibid
[11] Ibid.

the Netherlands State Commission, the matter will be referred to the Permanent Bureau for processing. The Permanent Bureau will then prepare a substantial memorandum or monograph involving necessary comparative research concerning the national laws of Member States in respect of the selected subjects. This is usually done by an expert comparative lawyer on the staff of the Bureau.[12] The research is usually assisted by the submission of questionnaires to the governments of the Member States. The replies to these questionnaires are to be analysed by the Permanent Bureau and circulated to all member governments after which a special commission of experts will be established for the preliminary discussion on the selected subjects.[13] The Commission of experts will arrange for the appointment of drafting committees and for the circulation of minutes and drafts to the members of the special commission and, subsequently to member states.

The task of this commission is to draft a Convention for the unification or harmonisation of law on the topic in issue on the basis of the available material and the desire of Member States. One notable thing about the work of the Commission is that since the members are usually experts in that particular field, political or national allegiance does not play a prominent role. The outcome of their practical work would be based on academic experience on the particular area of the law under consideration. The first draft of the Commission may be considered by a Member State on the basis of which more issues may be discussed, thereby calling for a re-consideration of the first draft of the commission. Since the taste of each government may be shown at this stage, political considerations may colour the views of the experts.

The final draft Convention will be submitted for the consideration of the plenary session of the Hague Conference. The Permanent Bureau has the responsibility of convening the Plenary Session of the Conference. It is also to see to its efficient administration, preparation and circulation of minutes, the circulation of the draft proposals and the successive drafts prepared by the drafting Committee.

---

[12] Ibid.
[13] Ibid.

At the Plenary Session, member states are expected to air their views on the political or economic effect, if any, of the Convention on their respective countries. At the end of the Plenary Conference, the Conventions and resolutions finally concluded by the delegates are gathered together in a final Act. This is then signed by the delegates. The signatures merely reflect the fact that the draft Conventions and resolutions which the Act contain are those agreed to by the delegates; they do not raise a presumption that the delegates' states approve or disapprove of the draft.

The Permanent Bureau is to later present the final product of the agreement of the Conference to Member States. This would be followed by the normal requirements of signature by the governments, ratification thereof and the eventual renunciation.

The work of the Hague Conference has had a tremendous impact on Private International Law. Several Conventions have been concluded[14] and many of them had been ratified by various countries.

International Institute for the Unification of Private Law (UNIDROIT)

The institute, with its headquarters at the Villa Aldobrandini, Rome, was founded and endowed by the Italian Government under the auspices of the League of Nations, and in close association with the organs of the League. The institute is presided over by a Governing Body appointed by the Council of the League.

When an issue is taken up by the Institute, it becomes the responsibility of the secretariat to collect all the information available as the law in force in the various countries. A comprehensive document usually called an "Etude" is prepared summarising the material collected to which is annexed the text, with a French translation attached, of the laws in force in various countries. The etudes is a comprehensive compilation of the laws in various jurisdictions and necessary information in respect of the work to be undertaken.

---

[14] Ibid.

A committee of experts would then consider the subject-matter. The committee is to endeavour to draft a uniform law.

The draft prepared by the committee of experts is to be sanitised by the Governing Body, and if approved, is sent to the council of the League at Geneva for such action as the council may deem fit to take.

The council of Europe

The Congress of Europe was held in The Hague in 1948. It was attended by representatives of twenty-four European States. The message to the European States read:

> We desire a United Europe, throughout whose area the free movement of persons, ideas and goods is restored; we desire a Charter of Human Rights guaranteeing liberty of thought, assembly and expression, a political opposition: we desire a court of Justice, with adequate sanctions for the implementation of this Charter: we desire a European Assembly where the live forces of all our nations shall be represented: and pledge ourselves... to give our fullest support to all persons and governments working for this lofty cause, which offers the last chance of peace and the one promise of a great future for this generation and those that will succeed it.[15]

The Council was constituted in 1949. It was made up of ten European States, with approximately 175 million citizens. It was established as a weak confederation of the nation States of Western Europe. It is now made up of not less than twenty-three non-communist European States with a total population of over 400 million citizens.[16]

The objective of the Council otherwise called "The Aim of the Council of Europe" can be found in Article I of its Statute. Article 1(a) states that it has the aim of achieving a greater unity between its

---

[15] Dowrick F.E. ``Juristic Activity in the Council of Europe - 25th Year" (1994) 23 *I.C.L.Q.* 610 at 611.

[16] Anton *op. cit.* p.48.

members.[17] The three fold tactical means of achieving this objective can be found in Article 1(b). The statute provides that this objective "shall be pursued through organs of the council

(a) by discussion of questions of common concern,
(b) by agreements and common action in administrative matters and
(c) in the maintenance and further realisation of human rights and fundamental freedoms."[18]

Issues of common concern are usually discussed by the Parliamentary Assembly, made up of members of the national parliaments of Member States, and a Committee of Ministers made up of a representative of the Government from each of the Member States. They have become regularly working European bodies over the years. The Consultative Assembly is made up of members of the Parliaments of all the Members States. They meet at least three times a year in Strasbourg. The Committee of Ministers comprising the Foreign Ministers of Member States (or their Deputies) meets monthly.

The juristic activities of the Council of Europe which it is proposed to consider usually owe their original impetus to a report or a debate in the Consultative Assembly; while the end-product, such as a draft Treaty or a settlement of a dispute, may eventually come before the Committee of Ministers. The most part of these juristic activities which relate to the drafting, interpreting and application of the laws are conducted by the subordinate bodies like the Legal Affairs Committee which is a Committee of the Consultative Assembly or the European Committee on Legal Co-operation or the European Committee on crime problems (groups of experts set up by the Committee of Ministers).

The function of the Committees of experts is to study problems in a wide range of matters and recommend to the appropriate body. The composition of a Committee depends on the subject-matter being dealt with. The Committee meets from time to time and makes a report. A

---

[17] The French states: "une union plus etroite entre ses members" This implies even closer bonds.
[18] See Dowrick *op. cit.* p.612.

draft Convention or a draft Recommendation (or resolution, so called until 1979) may be annexed thereto. It is usually required that a Recommendation or a draft Convention secures the unanimous agreement of the Committee of Ministers before it is passed or opened for signature. It has, however, been pointed out that it is technically possible for a draft Convention to be opened for signature by a two-thirds majority.[19]

The Directorate of Legal Affairs is a permanent administrative structure made up mainly of lawyers within the secretariat of the Council of Europe.

The Council of Europe has achieved much in the area of Human Rights. The basic Treaty, the Convention for the Protection of Human Rights and Fundamental Freedoms was signed in 1950 by all the then members of the Council of Europe. It entered into force on September 3, 1953 after it was ratified by 10 of the States. However by mid-1974 all the member states except one had ratified the Treaty. The Treaty defines in general terms a score of rights and freedoms for individuals, whether citizens or not, who are physically present in those states, or otherwise within their jurisdiction.

Under the original statute of the Council, neither the Consultative Assembly nor the Committee of Ministers was invested with legislative powers by Members States. In spite of this, the council of Europe has evolved its own "statute book" over the years. There are now in existence over 100 Conventions, Agreements and Protocols concluded between varying combinations of Member States and approved in their penultimate stage by the Committee of Ministers, at times by a two-thirds majority. They are not laws directly applicable within the territories of the member states in the way that Acts or Lois of national legislatures apply: nor are they directly applicable within all the legal systems of Member States in the manner that Regulations issued by the Commission and Council of the European Communities apply. However, in the Netherlands, where the monist theory of International law has penetrated into their national legal system, they are applicable.

---

[19] See Dowrick *op. cit.* 610 at 632; See also Anton *op. cit.* p.49

Where a Convention of the Council has been ratified, it forms part of International Treaty Law and as such they are expected to be implemented by internal measures.

The law emanating from the Council of Europe often spread over several years of preparatory work of committees operating under the aegies of the Council. The committee usually meet in Strasbourg. The power to transform the draft treaties into International Law resides in the states. This is done by ratification of the Convention.

The CCJ - Comite de Co-operation Juridique (European Co-operation) was set up by the Committee of Ministers in 1963 with the power to co-ordinate and to supervise the preparation of draft Conventions as well as model or uniform laws particularly in the fields of public and private international law and the private law of States. It is made up of delegates from each Member State, usually legal advisers from the respective foreign Ministers of Justice with rotating Chairmen. It has the power to reach decisions on matters of substance by a two-thirds majority. The basic preparation of each topic is carried out by sub-committees or by special committees of experts in that sphere. Where there is an agreement by the Committee of Ministers to open a draft Convention for signature by member states, it - i.e. the para-legislation, would then be on offer to member states for ratification.[20] Another way of going about it is through proposal from the annual sessions of the Ministers of Justice and from the occasional sessions of specialised ministers of all the member states.

From available records, as at 1 January 1987, a total of 123 draft Conventions and agreements (including several Protocols of earlier Conventions) have been approved by the Committee of Ministers and open for signature and ratification by member states. By this date, 103 had been ratified by the requisite minimum number of states to bring them into operation as binding international Treaties for those states. The draft Conventions face the usual slow process of ratification. The respective

---

[20] By virtue of Articles 15 and 20 of the Statute of the Council of Europe (1949), a decision to open a draft Convention for signature would be valid if approved by a two-thirds majority; a "political" way is through postponement of decisions; except if there is opposition by one or more member states. A draft Convention is signed by a majority vote of the Committee of Ministers.

governments are expected to pass necessary internal legislation implementing the Conventions if their law does not embody the requisite standards.

One thing of note is that some of these Conventions give allowance to states which are not members of the Council of Europe to accede to the Conventions. Thus, Finland,[21] Yugoslavia,[22] Israel,[23] Canada and U.S.A[24] have acceded to some of such Conventions. According to Dowrick, of the 123 drafts offered to member States by the Committee of Ministers since 1949, six (including the European Convention of Human Rights and its second Protocol) have been ratified by all 21 member states; four others by 20 member states; 52 others by ten or more states. He also noted that as at 1987, only 20 of these drafts have failed to secure sufficient ratifications over the years.[25]

Apart from Conventions, recommendations also form another method of harmonisation of laws by the Council of Europe. Recommendations usually emanate from the Committee of Ministers addressed to member States' governments and are also authorised by the Statute of Europe. In a way, the recommendations (until 1979 called Resolutions) are legal instruments issued by the Council of Europe. They do not refuse states' imprimatur to confer that status on them and they do not bind member states. They evolve from the committees of the council first as the draft Conventions and they need the unanimous approval of the Committee of Ministers.

Recommendations usually contain proposals for harmonising laws or administrative measures. Various recommendations are usually issued by the Committee of Ministers. This power is usually used in the sphere of criminal law and penal affairs on the basis of drafts produced by the

---

[21] Finland had ratified among others, Conventions relating to conservation of Wildlife and the Cultural Conventions.

[22] Yugoslavia had also ratified among others Conventions relating to higher education diplomas.

[23] Israel has ratified at least three of the Conventions.

[24] In respect of Canada and the United States of America, the Convention on the Transfer of Sentenced Persons among others may be mentioned.

[25] Dowrick *op. cit.*

C.D.C.P.[26]

The European Economic Community (EEC)

Following the endorsement of the Spaak Report by the Government of the six, two Treaties were signed in Rome on March 25, 1957 providing for the establishment of a European Economic Community, and a European Atomic Energy Community. These Treaties became operational on January 1, 1958. A Convention was also signed contemporaneously with the founding Treaties providing for a single Assembly and court of Justice for the EEC and Euratom.

Following the creation of the EEC, Austria, Denmark, Norway, Sweden, Switzerland, Portugal and the United Kingdom signed the Stockholm Convention on January 4, 1960, and thereby created the European Free Trade Association (EFTA) in May 1960.

The EFTA countries otherwise called the "Outer Seven" had as its primary object the objective of offsetting any detrimental progressive elimination of tariffs by the community by a similar reduction within the EFTA. It was also believed that the EFTA should be regarded as a stepping stone to possible future membership of the EEC. It is instructive to note that this belief is coming to pass because despite the initial refusal to allow some EFTA states to join the EEC, several of them are now members of this body.

As a result of the creation of the EEC, Austria, Denmark, Norway, Sweden, Switzerland, Portugal and the United Kingdom signed the Stockholm Convention on January 4, 1960, and thereby creating the European Free Trade Association (EFTA) in May 1960.

The objective of the EFTA countries otherwise called the "Outer

---

[26] See for example, Protocols on the Extradition Treaty, No 86: Additional Protocol (1975) to the European Convention on Extradition No 24 of 1957; No 98: Second Additional Protocol to the above (1978); Protocol on the European Court of Human Rights abolishing the death penalty except in times of war or imminent threat of war, No 14; Protocol. No. 6 to the Convention on Human Rights concerning the Abolition of the Death Penalty (1983).

Seven" was to offset any detrimental effects to their trade resulting from the progressive elimination of tariffs by the Community by a similar reduction within the EFTA. It should however be pointed out that EFTA was regarded as a stepping stone to possible future membership of the EEC. This belief is coming to pass because despite the initial refusal to allow some of the EFTA states to join the EEC, several of them are now members of the EEC.

Historically, the term "European Community" indicates a vague idea of Western European Unity. In actual fact however, one needs to speak of three communities. These are the Coal and Steel Community, the Atomic Energy Community, and the Economic Community. In practical terms, these three juristic communities reflect different economic functions. Despite the difference in respect of their Treaties, they all have the same executive, administrative, legislative and judicial character. Thus, they use the same parliament, Commission, Council of Ministers and Court of Justice, although the performance of their duties is in accordance with their respective Treaties. Attention shall be focused on the European Economic Community.

The European Community is a developed legal organisation which is federal in nature. The structure of the community legal order can be considered from the following angles. The first relates to the doctrine of direct applicability or direct effect of laws. The other deals with the supremacy of community law. These are the usual doctrines of international law. As pointed out above the nature of the relationship between the Community law and national law is like that between the state and federal law in a federal system. It seems however that the federal/state analogy cannot be driven too far. For example, it cannot be said that the exclusive and concurrent legislative lists which are usually present in national laws or constitution can be found in the Community law relations with national laws.. It seems that in the normal course of events, where a national law is inconsistent with a community law, the national law must give way. For example, in *Simmenthal*,[27] the court held that Community law was competent to "preclude the valid

---

[27] [1978] E.C.R 629; [1978] 3C.M.L.R. 263.

adoption" of inconsistent national legislation.

The legislative power of the community

The Council has the power to enact legislation for the purpose of achieving the objectives of the Treaty. This power is also possessed, in a lesser degree, by the Commission. Article 189 provides:

> In order to carry out their task, the Council and the Commission shall, in accordance with the provisions of this Treaty, make Regulations, issue directives, take decisions, make recommendations, or deliver opinions.

Treaties

This is the usual way of making laws in the supra-national context. A Treaty is the law incorporating the agreement of member states in respect of a particular subject matter. The most popular Treaty seems to be that on Jurisdiction and Enforcement of Foreign Judgements otherwise called the Brussels Convention. This Convention determines the jurisdiction of the court in respect of matters to be litigated. For example, under the English national law, once a defendant is served with the writ of summons or if he is present within the jurisdiction of the court, the court may assume jurisdiction over the matter. The Brussels Convention however uses domicile as the connecting factor in issues relating to jurisdiction and enforcement of judgments. Where a draft Treaty is ratified and acceded to by the Member States, it becomes binding on them. All the Member States are expected to abide with the provisions of the Treaty.

Where a Community legislation is inconsistent with rules of international law, which ordinarily should be binding on the community, that legislation to the extent of its inconsistency is void.

Regulations

Article 189 of the Treaty provides: "A Regulation shall have general application. It shall be binding in its entirety and directly applicable in all Member States."

Regulations have direct effect and as such are right conferring and this must be protected by nation states. It is not necessary, indeed it has been said that it is not permissible to have national implementation instruments before a Regulation would be considered as binding. As such, it has been stated that unless authorised in a particular case, it should not be derogated from. In *Krohn case*,[28] the court acknowledged that where Community Regulations require implementation by national measures, the incorporation of the texts of such Regulations may be justified for the sake of coherence and in order to make them comprehensive to the persons to whom they apply.

Since Regulations constitute direct legislation by the Community, not only may individuals rely on specific provisions as against other individuals and member states, they may also invoke the general objective and purpose Regulations as against national legal provisions. In effect, it is possible to invoke the encroachment by national legislation on an area of community competence.

In *Amsterdam Bulb Bv* v *Produktschap Voor Siergewassen Case*,[29] the court stated:

> From the moment that the Community adopts Regulations under Article 40 in a specific sector the Member States are under a duty not to take any measure which might create exemptions from them or affect them adversely. The compatibility with the Community Regulations of the provisions referred to by the national court must be considered in the light not only of the express provisions of the Regulations but also of their aims and objectives.

Directives and decisions

Articles 189 provides:

---

[28] Case 74/69 [1970] E.C.R 451.
[29] Case 50/76 [1977] E.C.R. 137 at 147.

> A directive shall be binding, as to the result to be achieved, upon each member state to which it is addressed but shall leave to the national authorities the choice of form and methods.
>
> A decision shall be binding in its entirety upon those to whom it is addressed.

The following should be noted.

1. A directive may be addressed only to a state. It may also be addressed to a natural or legal person.
2. A decision addressed to a member state, by contrast, would be an act of the Commission requiring a Member state to abolish or amend measures of aid to national undertakings.
3. The choice of form and methods for the implementation of directives allows member states to choose the legislative format ·which it considers appropriate.
4. Directives do not require legislative implementation where there exist general principles of constitutional or administrative law which render specific legislation superfluous, provided that these principles guarantee the application of the directive and they are clear and precise and are made known to those subject to the law, and are capable of being invoked in the courts.
5. Directives are capable of vesting rights in individuals which national courts are bound to safeguard. In *Duyn* v *Home Office*, the court held that Article 3(1) of Directive 64/22/ gave rise to rights in individuals which national courts were bound to safeguard.

It needs be emphasised that harmonisation of laws is a good idea in bringing promotion of commerce and co-existence. The efforts of the bodies herein discussed and others should be commended. A lot can still be done to bring about desired uniformity as opposed to the present chaos of rules.

4

The African Economic Treaty

Africa is made up of not less than 51 countries.[1] It is a developing continent with diverse resources and problems. It is a continent for the future in the sense that most of the countries that make up the continent are still grappling with various internal and externally induced problems. The problems could be classified as economic, political, social and legal.

Up till recently, Africa was regarded as a dark continent in the sense that it was basically undeveloped and unknown. A traverse in Africa by any. discoverer, in the time past, was usually regarded as a tread in the jungle. This notion has even continued till today. This is due to lack of sufficient literature on Africa and the Africans. This is also true of the African legal systems. In respect of our laws, it was believed that we did not have any law and that if there were social norms for the regulation of inter-personal relationships, they were not sufficiently developed to qualify as laws properly so called.[2]

With time, and the advent of the Europeans in large numbers for the purpose of colonisation or conquest of many of the countries that make up Africa, the social values and institutions of Africans became recognised and appreciated. Nevertheless, it was felt that the recognition and enforcement of such African laws must pass the test of civilised notions of justice.[3] Even when allowance was made for the operation of our laws especially by the British, it was felt that it was impracticable to totally reject the established African institutions. Lord Lugard once

---

[1] See Times Books London - *The Times Atlas of the World* (1980) pg. 7.

[2] See M.A. Ajomo in *Integration of the African Continent through Law* (Min. of Justice Publication) p.100 at 102.

[3] See generally I.O., Agbede, *Themes on Conflict of Laws* A.O. Obilade, *The Nigerian Legal System* A.W. Park *Sources of Nigerian Law.*

pointed out that it was unwise

> ...to forego the high ideal of leading the backward races, by their own efforts, in their own way to raise themselves to a higher plane of social organisation.[4]

In summary, it was felt that the recognition and enforcement of such African laws must pass the test of civilised notions of justice, in the language of the laws of most English speaking African countries, the customary laws could only be recognised and enforced if such laws did not contradict notions of natural justice, equity - not necessarily in the abstract, good conscience and public policy - with the attendant problem of definition. To the French, the local laws must not be *contraire aux principle de la civilisation Francaise.*[5]

Of course, the customary laws could not present the necessary anecdote for regulating social affairs of men. Foreign laws were thus introduced and such laws are usually referred to as the general law.[6] Various foreign legal systems have therefore taken root in Africa. Such foreign legal systems include French, English, Spanish, Roman-Dutch systems among others. Each country has its own version of imported general law.

Then the question may be asked, when a developing continent, such as Africa, over-burdened by external debts and manipulations, self-induced problems and/or factors has to think of development, there must be co-operation among them. More often than not, the strength of a nation, and, *afortiori*, a continent is usually determined by its economy. Many African countries have stories of economic woes to tell.[7] It is in

---

[4] O.I. Agbede, *Legal Pluralism* (Shaneson) p.6

[5] See M.A. Ajomo *op. cit.* p. 100

[6] This law is general' in the sense that it applies to all, it does not take into account race, colour or the accidental place of birth. This is unlike the customary law which attaches to a person by reason of the fact that that person is a member of that particular community.

[7] Many African nations are indebted to international financial bodies like the World Bank and the International Monetary Fund. The inability of many

the light of this that the African Economic Treaty is of paramount importance given the greater economic co-operation among the countries of Europe and American states.

The basis of African Economic Treaty

The basis of the African Economic Treaty is co-operation among the African countries for the purpose of bringing about economic buoyancy to African nations. Before a detailed analysis and importance of the African Economic Treaty in particular is embarked upon, it is necessary to discuss the importance of international economic co-operation in general.

Importance of international economic co-operation: harmonisation/unification of laws

It is beyond argument that no nation, so to speak, is an island, hence the need for co-operation among various nations of the world. The interaction of human beings beyond border lines calls for the recognition of rules to regulate inter-personal relationships. This is usually done through harmonisation of laws and institutions.

Harmonisation brings about practical and predictable rules for the determination of the appropriate law to apply in the resolution of practical problems on uniform basis.[8] The diverse legal systems in Africa is a consequence of the colonial history of the continent. With the harmonisation of the legal web which the various legal systems could be called, commerce will be enhanced and the economy of the African

---

African nations to pay their debts usually result in the prescription of bitter pills of economic reforms or regulations like Structural Adjustment Programme (SAP) or counter-trade. Recent developments in countries like Ghana and Nigeria show such prescriptions are usually against the interest of such African nations.

[8] Since uniformity brings about certainty, the determination of the law at a point in time and the possibility of projecting into the future is to be preferred.

nations will be improved.

Economic co-operation enhances the inter-play of legal collaboration[9] and mutual respect between nations that would otherwise suffer from mutual economic suspicion and war. This is more important in Africa where a little spark could cause a great conflagration due to mutual suspicion among the nations. The various choice of law rules in the area of commerce have proved inadequate or inappropriate necessitating further and better co-operation. It is possible for some nations to take a myopic view of harmonisation as an indirect way of giving up their sovereignty. Instead of looking at harmonisation from this angle, it should rather be regarded as a step in the search for certainty in the law and the promotion of international commerce and co-existence. The adoption of this method will bring about the convergence of various legal systems [10]. The benefits derivable from legal co-operation among nations cannot be over-emphasised. Modern global commercial network has shown that the various choice of law rules are unsuitable for international cooperation. The other benefits derivable from economic cooperation from the legal perspective could be summarised as follows! Where there is legal cooperation, it would be possible to have unity of connecting factors. This would bring about certainty in the law and the possibility of giving accurate advice to clients.

It would also be possible to enforce the judgments of one country in another since it may not be necessary to have agreements or Conventions on recognition and enforcement of foreign judgments.

Legal cooperation does not necessarily create a situation where one of the contracting states would state in helplessness: "my hands are tied". There is always the retention of power to opt out of the law which would otherwise apply if such would not be in the interest of that

---

[9] See Koopmans T., "The Birth of European Law At the Cross Roads of Legal Traditions" (1991) 39 *Am. J.C.L.* 493.

[10] The position of the EEC in this regard is a classical example of the convergence of various legal systems for the purpose of achieving uniformity in the laws of member states in respect of the issues which are agreed upon.

particular contracting state.

There is nothing as suitable as having a single court for the resolution of matters which may be of common interest. Harmonisation of laws and the establishment of a uniform appellate court encourages uniform interpretation of concepts and issues which may arise under the Convention.

It is beyond doubt that even where harmonisation exists, each country will still retain its legal system. The advantage of this setting is that there would be convergence of various legal traditions and the consequent enrichment of the respective legal systems.

Even where legal cooperation is on a particular issue like commerce, it would also have some effect on other aspects of a nation's existence as that portion alone cannot exist in vacuo.

Public policy exists to stop or disallow the application of an otherwise applicable law. This concept has been described as an unruly horse. It can be invoked to frustrate the reasonable expectation of parties. Where uniform laws exist its application would be irrelevant or at least reduced to the barest minimum.

Harmonisation encourages the development of autonomous jurisprudence through a cosmopolitan approach to the interpretation of principles and concepts.

This idea also has the effect of reducing the problem of the forum to litigate or what may be termed litigation about where to litigate.

Harmonisation brings about certainty in the law. When the law is certain it would be respected and this would be good for the legal system and the stability of the government.

Since legal cooperation brings nations together, this would enhance the spirit of brotherliness among member states.

This idea also makes it possible to have a uniform reach to other legal traditions especially those that are outside the continent.

Where several countries stay together for a particular purpose, there is the consequent respect which they would earn from countries outside this cooperation as other countries would appreciate the possibility of oneness in spite of their difference.

The advantages derivable from this idea can be multiplied. It must however not be imagined that once there is cooperation, then each country will not have the opportunity of protecting its own valued principles. Within the precincts of legal cooperation, there would still be opportunity to make reservations. It should however be pointed out that economic issues do not always succumb to emotional issues which matters relating to culture or social institutions are susceptible.

From the resume of advantages of commercial cooperation highlighted above, it would be seen that legal cooperation is better than a cacophony of rules. Indeed, legal cooperation avoids the costly, confusion and delay fluently illustrated by Lando, will therefore often feel the same frustration as did Voltaire, when he travelled to France, where the law changed every time he changed horses.[11]

Lessons from other jurisdictions

International legal cooperation has become part of the European legal culture. International bodies have been set up to help in the realisation of this objective. Such bodies include the Unidroit, the Hague Conference on Private International Law, the Uncitraal, the EEC and the Council of Europe. In respect of America, one can talk of the Organisation of American States.

This Chapter shall discuss briefly the significance of the EEC Convention on Jurisdiction and Enforcement of Judgments otherwise called the Brussels Convention. This Convention regulates the daily problem of jurisdiction which is the foundation of any adjudication. It also deals with the recognition and enforcement of foreign judgments. A judgement deserves that appellation only when it can be recognised and its utility depends on whether it could be enforced as such.

Prior to the EEC Civil Jurisdiction and Judgments Convention, each country comprising the EEC had its own rules relating to recognition and enforcement of judgments. For the purpose of history as far as the European countries are concerned and for the benefit of African nations, as each country has its own rules in this respect, the position of the law

---

[11] See Lando O. *International Contracts and Conflict of Laws* (Sarv.) p.2

in some European countries will now be undertaken.

In France, prior to 1964, the practice was to review the judgment of a foreign court whose enforcement was sought within jurisdiction.[12] In 1964, following the decision of the court in *Munzer* v *Dame Munzer*[13] it was established that the requirement for recognition should not relate to the review of a case as regards the merit thereof but should be based on whether necessary procedure was followed by the adjudicating court.

Like the position under the French Law, it was not necessary to have a formal reciprocal legislation before the judgment of a foreign court could be recognised in Belgium. As a Belgian court pointed out:

> After examination of all the main claims which initially were submitted to the foreign court and all the legal and factual circumstances which determined the decision of the court, the Belgian court grants or refuses, in full or part, the recognition without, in substance, having the power to substitute its own decision for that of the foreign court.[14]

Unlike the French court however, the Belgian judge was not obliged to verify whether the foreign judgment was reached the way a Belgian court will determine it and it was not for the Belgian judge to verify whether the appropriate substantive law was invoked by the adjudicating court.

German law required a reciprocal arrangement before the judgment of a foreign court can be recognised. This was not required under the French, Belgian, Italian and Dutch practices. This made recognition and enforcement difficult. The requirement of reciprocity did not apply to claims which did not involve property or where the person was not connected with Germany.[15]

---

[12] See G.J. Roman, *Recognition and Enforcement of Foreign Judgements in various Foreign Countries* (1984) p.5

[13] Juris-Casseur Periodique (J.C.P) 1964, 13590 cited in G.J. Roman *op. cit.* 5

[14] Court Civile de Bruxelles, February 18, 1939 cited in G. J. Roman *op. cit.* p. 14.

[15] See G. Beitzke, "Reconnaisance at execution des decisions judiciares entrangeres dans la Republique Federale d'Allenmangne" 7 Rivista di Diritto

One thing which must however be said is that nearly all jurisdictions . required that the judgment must be given by a court of competent jurisdiction, that the parties must be heard and that the matter must be conclusive. It must also be devoid of collusion or fraud. The reason for these requirements was that since the recognising court was required to treat the judgment as its own, the requirements of justice in a civilised society should be observed.

In respect of the connecting factors, some European countries required domicile as the connecting factor. Nationality was required by some others. England and its former territories required service of the writ or voluntary submission to the jurisdiction of the court except in the case of out-of-service jurisdiction which was and still is discretionary.

Under the current Convention, domicile is the connecting factor. This is a welcome development. It seems that domicile is more apposite in this respect than the idea of nationality since nationality may be of little or no importance to men of commerce.

This Convention is a by-product of the co-operation between some European nations to have uniform rules to govern issues relating to the international jurisdiction of the courts and to hear cases and enforce foreign judgments in civil and commercial matters. This Convention was signed at Brussels on behalf of the six original member states of the EEC on 22 September 1968. A unique feature of this Convention is that it was the first of the community Convention in this area of the law to enter into force as a result of its ratification by the six initial member states pursuant to Articles 61 and 62 of the Convention. The expression "civil and commercial matters" in this context as interpreted in *Eurocontrol*[16] is not confined to the meaning given to it by the courts of a state. The Convention is usually interpreted "by reference, first to the objectives and schemes of the Convention and, secondly, to the general principles which stem from the corpus of the national legal systems."[17]

Interia-Zionale Private e Processuale 242 (1971) cited in G.J. Roman *op. cit.* p. 19.
[16] (1976) ECR 1541
[17] Ibid. at 1552-53

The Convention applies to all issues except:

i. The status or legal capacity of natural persons, rights in property arising out of a matrimonial relationship, wills and succession.
ii. Bankruptcy, proceedings relating to the winding up of insolvent companies or other legal persons, judicial arrangements, compositions and analogous proceedings.
iii. Social Security
iv. Arbitration[18]

The European court of Justice serves as the clearing house in respect of appeals emanating from the member states of the EEC.

With the benefit of hindsight, the Brussels Convention is one of the successful attempts at legal co-operation or harmonisation of laws.

The African Economic Community Treaty Preliminaries

The African Economic Community Treaty is a by-product of several years of efforts at continental cooperation. It is common to mention the OAU meeting held at Algiers in 1968 as the place of the birth of this idea. This was followed by the Monrovia summit of 1979 which led to the Monrovia Declaration. In 1980, at the Lagos Economic summit, this idea was concretised and it finally led to the Final Act of Lagos.[19]

Prior to the agreement on African economic cooperation, the Organisation of African Unity (OAU) charter had made provisions for this idea.[20] For example, the third preambular paragraph of the OAU Charter emphasises the need

> To harness the natural and human resources of our continent for the total advancement of our peoples in spheres of human endeavours.

It's ninth pre-ambular paragraph states the determination of "all

---

[18] See Article 1(2) of the Convention
[19] This Treaty was signed on the 3rd day of June 1991.
[20] See the last three paragraphs of the Preamble

African states (to) henceforth unite so that the welfare and well-being of (the) peoples may be assured".

In response to this, the preamble to the Treaty states the basis for establishing the African Economic union.[21] It states *inter alia.*

> NOTING that the efforts already made in sub-regional and regional sectoral economic cooperation are encouraging and justify a larger and fuller economic integration;
>
> NOTING the need to share, in an equitable and just manner the advantages of cooperation among member states in order to promote a balanced economic development in all parts of the continent.
>
> Have decided to establish an African Economic Community constituting an integral part of the OAU....

This preamble notes past efforts at regional cooperation and appreciates the fact that this idea can bring about a balanced economic development. The community is to operate as part of the Organisation of African Unity which is the umbrella body that brings together the African nations for the purpose of discussing and solving various problems besetting the African continent.

Articles 3-5 state the basic principles behind the establishment of the community. Basically, this Treaty is to see to the mutual understanding, cooperation and recognition of rights of the member states. It is also to promote the economic, social and cultural development and for the integration of African economies for the purpose of increasing economic self-reliance and self-sustained development. For the purpose of attaining these objectives the community is to ensure the strengthening of existing regional communities since it is easier to discuss and implement agreements on regional basis than on a continental scale.

Another important method of achieving the objectives is through the liberalisation of trade through the abolition, among member states, of customs duties levied on imports and exports and the abolition of non-tariff barriers for the purpose of establishing a free trade area at the level

---

[21] See Article 4 of the Treaty.

of each regional economic community. The benefit of this is that liberal trade laws would necessarily ensure free movement of goods and capital and thereby create a rich network of commerce. The community is also to ensure the establishment and maintenance of a common external tariff.[22]

Even among the African states, the Treaty recognises that some can be classified as least developed.[23] It therefore recommends the adoption of special measures in favour of land-locked, semi-land locked and Island countries. It also encourages the establishment of institutions and organs for the purpose of attaining these objectives.[24] It should be pointed out that these objectives are to be achieved in stages.[25] Indeed, Article 6 specifically states that the Community shall be established gradually in six stages of variable duration over a transitional period not exceeding thirty-four years. This Article also states what is to be achieved at each stage of the transitional period. The various organs of the community are mentioned in Article 7.

The supreme organ of the community is the Assembly of Heads of State and Government.[26] It is given the power to implement the objectives of the community in all ramifications.[27] The Assembly is expected to meet once a year in regular session but an extra-ordinary session may be convened by the chairman of the Assembly following a request by two-thirds of the members of the Assembly.[28]

The functions and development of the community are to be carried out by an organ - the council of ministers of the OAU. This idea is in line with the resolution that the OAU and the community be merged into one organisation with a single secretariat.[29]

---

[22] See generally Article 4 of the Treaty

[23] See Articles 4(k) and 78 of the Treaty

[24] See Article 4 (m) of the Treaty

[25] See Article 6 of the Treaty

[26] See Article 7 of the Treaty

[27] See Article 7(2) of the Treaty

[28] See Article 8 of the Treaty

[29] See Resolution AHG/Res. 190 (xxxvi). This conclusion was based on political and foundational considerations.

The Treaty proposes the establishment of a Pan-African parliament whose primary function is to ensure that the peoples of Africa are fully involved in the economic development and integration of the continent.[30]

It is an objective of the Treaty that a court like the European court of Justice should be established for the purpose of deciding disputes submitted to it.[31]

The Secretary-General who is to direct the activities of the secretariat shall also be its legal representative.[32] He, as well as his assistants, are to be elected by the Assembly in accordance with the relevant provisions of the OAU Charter and the rules of procedure of the Assembly.[33] The Treaty requires absolute loyalty on the part of its functionaries and requests that they shall neither seek nor accept instructions from any Government or any national or international authority to the Community. The basis of this provision is to prevent divided loyalty on the part of the Community.[34]

Chapter five which contains fourteen Articles deals with customs union,[35] duties,[36] non-tariff barriers to intra-community trade[37] and the establishment of a common external customs tariff.[38] It also deals with the system of intra-community trade,[39] internal taxes,[40] prohibition of dumping within the community re-export of goods[41] and intra-community transit facilities[42] customs cooperation administration,[43]

---

[30] See Article 14 of the Treaty.
[31] See Article 17 of the Treaty.
[32] See Article 22 of the Treaty.
[33] See Article 23 of the Treaty.
[34] See Article 24(1) of the Treaty.
[35] See Article 29 of the Treaty.
[36] See Article 30 of the Treaty.
[37] See Article 31 of the Treaty.
[38] See Article 32 of the Treaty.
[39] See Article 33 of the Treaty.
[40] See Article 34 of the Treaty.
[41] See Article 36 of the Treaty.
[42] See Article 38 of the Treaty.

trade documents and procedures,[44] compensatory exchange agreement and trade promotion.[45] This chapter has as its desiratum the elimination of barriers or inhibitions to trade and fiscal issues. It also deals with regulation of goods and trade at the international level.[46]

The Treaty also affirms the need to promote freedom of movement of persons, rights of residence and establishment among other inalienable rights.[47]

Like the attempt of the European countries to have a common currency in line with the Machrist Treaty, Article 44[48] goes the mid-way by providing that member states shall harmonise their monetary, financial and payment policies in order to boost intra-community trade in goods and services and their national currencies are to be used in the settlement of commercial and financial transactions in order to reduce the use of external currencies in such transactions. To facilitate this, clearing mechanisms among the different regions are to be integrated into an African clearing and Payment house and it is proposed that in the final analysis, an African Monetary union is to be established through the harmonisation of regional monetary zones.[49]

There are also provisions for free movement of capital through the elimination of restrictions on the transfer of capital funds between member states.[50] Other provisions include those on development of agriculture in all ramifications,[51] industry, science, technology, energy, natural resources, environment[52], transport,[53] communication[54] and

---

[43] See Article 39 of the Treaty.
[44] See Article 40 of the Treaty.
[45] See Articles 41 & 42 of the Treaty.
[46] See for example Article 42 (ii) of the Treaty.
[47] See Article 43 of the Treaty.
[48] That is, Article 44 (g).
[49] See Article 44 (g).
[50] Article 45
[51] Chapter VIII
[52] Chapter IX
[53] Article 61
[54] Article 61

tourism.[55] There are also provisions on posts and telecommunication,[56] broadcasting,[57] tourism[58] standardization and measurement systems[59] and education, training, culture,[60] human resources,[61] social affairs,[62] health,[63] population,[64] women and development.[65]

Chapter 18 deals with the establishment of a continental court of Justice for the purpose of settling disputes. Chapters 19-21 which contain eight Articles encourage or promote interaction between the community and regional economic communities, African continental organisations, African non-Governmental Organisations and socio-economic organisations and associations as well as third states and international organisations.

Withdrawal from the community is possible.[66] Any member state that wishes to withdraw from the community must give a year notice in writing to the Secretary General. When this is done, the secretary shall inform the member states of this development.

The Treaty was drawn up in four original texts in the Arabic, English, French and Portuguese languages. The four texts are regarded as authentic.[67]

The African Economic Treaty is a bold step in continental co-operation. It takes a peep into the future but whether the aims and objectives of the Treaty would be achieved within the time frame stipulated in the Treaty is another matter entirely. In view of this, it is

---

[55] Article 61
[56] Article 63
[57] Article 64
[58] Article 65
[59] Chapter XI
[60] Article 70
[61] Article 71
[62] Article 72
[63] Article 73
[64] Article 74
[65] Article 75
[66] Article 104
[67] Article 106

necessary to consider the problems which may arise in the implementation of the provisions of this Treaty.

Implementation of the provisions of the African Economic Treaty - probable problems

The first issue which must be considered is the improbability of achieving the highlighted objectives within the time frame stipulated for the diverse issues raised in the Treaty. A particular objective may leap into the time frame meant for the achievement of another and at the end of the day, little achievement may be recorded.

Leadership problem may also hinder the achievement of the objectives of the community. A selfish leader may not mind sacrificing the interest of the community for the achievement of his own selfish objective. It is a known fact that there are many sit-tight presidents and heads of states in Africa. Such leaders would rather sacrifice the interest of the people in order to maintain the hide and seek game necessary for their own survival.

Socio-cultural differences among African nations should also be considered. Where there is a pronounced socio-cultural divide, it may stall the achievement of the enviable objectives of the community.

The community will also have to contend with linguistic and political problems. It has also been pointed out that the existence of border conflicts and racial suspicion on the continent between black Africans and Arab Africans can hamper economic integration.[68] It is doubtful whether many African leaders would be willing to implement the programmes of the community even if this would jeopardise the singular interest of their respective countries.

It is beyond doubt that the laudable objectives of the community can only be attained in a stable continent. It is a known fact that many

---

[68] See Ndulo M., The Promotion of Intra-African Trade and The Harmonisation of laws in the African Economic Community: Prospects and Problems, *African Economic Community Treaty Issues, Problems and Prospects*, (1993) p. 107.

African countries are not stable. A country that has to contend with civil strife cannot have the time or the commitment to observe and enforce the provisions of the Treaty.

Although there is provision for the establishment of an International Court of Justice, problem of personnel and the enforcement of the judgment of that court may affect the efficiency of such judgments.

Furthermore, it should be pointed out that the independence of the judiciary is usually determined by adequate funding. The proposed activities of this court may be stalled by financial constraints. Indeed, the probable problems which may besiege the community can be multiplied. In spite of the above however, it is a good thing that there is a Community Treaty in Africa that attempts to bring together African nations for the purpose of developing the continent.

The success recorded by some European countries through legal cooperation shows that if the provisions of the Treaty are properly implemented much could be achieved. The need for cooperation among the African nations is more pronounced given the fact that many of our people still wallow in abject poverty and squalor. The Treaty contains viable and valuable provisions. The idea of legal co-operation may reduce the problem of the existing diverse legal systems which exist in the continent. One noticeable omission is the non-provision of a specialised committee to deal with legal issues.[69] In view of the fact that Article 25(2) gives the Assembly the power to restructure the existing committees, it is hereby suggested that provisions should be made for the establishment of a committee to deal with legal issues.

African universities should also deem it necessary to give attention

---

[69] Article 25 which deals with the establishment of various specialised technical committees does not mention the establishment of a legal committee. Those mentioned are: (I) The Committee on Rural Economy and Agricultural Matter; (ii) The Committee on Monetary and Financial Affairs (iii) The Committee on Trade, Customs and Immigration Matters; (iv) The Committee on Industry, Science and Technology, Energy, Natural Resources and Environment, (v) The Committee on Transport, Communications and Tourism (vi) The Committee on Health Labour and Social Affairs; and (vii) The Committee on Education, Culture and Human Resources.

to legal cooperation. Comparative studies should also be emphasised as part of the Legal Education of the university students.

For now, what is required is honesty of purpose among African leaders and those who are saddled with the responsibility of ensuring the implementation of the provisions of the Treaty. If the provisions of the Treaty are objectively pursued it may be the beginning of economic opulence and the consequent dawn of a new era for the countries that make up Africa.

5

Relations between the African economic community and the African regional communities

International economic relations have revealed that the best method of acquiring economic power is through the convergence of resources and economic activities, after all, no nation is self-sufficient, and in any event, political power without a virile economy means little or nothing. There is therefore, the need to transfer part of each nation's sovereignty, so to speak, to a body whose power is beyond the confines of each nation's boundaries. The above reasons have therefore led to the formation and recognition of the continental and regional economic communities. The reasons for the establishment of a supra-national body to protect the interest of the African economy could be gathered from Article 4 of the African Economic Treaty (AET). It states in part:

The objectives of the community shall be

(a) to promote economic, social and cultural development and the integration of African economies in order to increase economic self-reliance and promote an indigenous and self-sustained development;

(b) to establish, on a continental scale, a framework for the development, mobilisation and utilisation of the human and material resources of Africa in order to achieve a self-reliant development;

(c) to promote co-operation in all fields of human endeavour in order to raise the standard of living of African people, and maintain and enhance economic stability, foster close and peaceful relations among member states and contribute to the progress, development and the economic integration of the continent; and

(d) to co-ordinate and harmonise policies among existing and future economic communities in order to foster the gradual establishment of the community.

The AET realises the importance of the regional bodies which have been in existence before its formation hence the provision that the existing regional economic communities shall be strengthened. The Treaty further enjoins the establishment of such sectoral economic bodies where they do not exist. Various regional bodies like the Economic Community of West African States (ECOWAS), the East African Community (EAC), the South African Development Co-ordination Conference (SADCC), the Preferential Trade Area (PTA) and the African Economic Treaty (AET) are now in place. The probable difficulties and conflicts which may arise by reason of this integration shall be the focus of this chapter, but before a discussion on this is embarked upon, certain issues must be discussed.

Factors leading to continental and regional integration in Africa

Integration relates to any process leading to the formation of a political and economic whole or an organised unit. It has been noted that integration problems arise as a result of economic activities which are not organised on a global level. The need for integration emerged out of a disorderly process resulting from the push of spontaneous economic activities and spontaneous growth and from the random waves of local power seizure, conquest and national liberation.[1]

The much expected independence attained by various African nations did not bring about enough succour or comfort.[2] Doubtless, such could not be attained given the fact that independence *per se* does not

---

[1] *Economic Integration: Concepts, Theories and Problems* Ed. Mihaly Simai & Katalin Garman (Akad. Kiado Budapest 1977) p. 41.

[2] Various African countries attained independence at various periods. For example, Ghana got her Independence in 1957 while Nigeria got her Independence in 1960.

bring about opulence without necessary political will, viable economy, abundant resources, courageous and incorruptible leadership. It has therefore been realised that much could be achieved through co-operation. An integration process therefore is not more than the process of sharing valued economic system or the process of putting more or less explicitly on record some fundamental norms for economic activity and in delineating the area for which they are valid.

An integration process may be intensive or extensive. An intensive one bears on working out and reinforcing the norms of the systems, while an extensive one bears on defining and widening the political and economic space governed by those norms.[3] Either has in focus joint developmental efforts.

Africa is blessed with various mineral resources.[4] The continent retains the following shares of world resources: Diamond 19%, Choromite 80%, Cobalt 70%, Bauxite 50%, Gold 50%, Phosphate Rock 50%, Iron Ore 45%, Uranium 40%, Tantalite 40%, Copper 25%, Manganese Ore 20% and Tin 16% among other resources. A lot will be lost through divergent economic policies. Co-operation can definitely bring about comparison of notes, advice, admonition, help and collaboration in various ways.

It should be emphasised that pristine national sovereignty claim and non-interference in the internal affairs of other nations' principle can have no pride of place[5] especially when many African nations approach, most of the time, cap in hand, international financial institutions like the World Bank and the International Monetary Fund (I. M. F.) for aid.

The erstwhile *laissez faire* doctrine was hallowed as a manifestation of freedom. It soon became apparent to weaker independent African nations that *laissez faire* policies more often than not benefit economically strong nations at the expense of those that are weak.[6]

---

[3] Abique M., *The Development of African Economic Underdevelopment* p. 8.

[4] *Ibid.* p. 40

[5] See *Readings and Documents on ECOWAS* published by: The Nigerian Institute of International Affairs (1983).

[6] Note the views of classical thinkers like Adam Smith, Jeremy Bentham, James Mills and John Stuart Mill.

Therefore, with the benefit of hindsight, events from other territories and the proverbial brotherly affection, African nations have decided to legislate and collaborate at supra national level to protect weaker nations under the umbrella of the Organisation of African Unity and the African Economic Treaty.[7] For example, the African Economic Treaty states as one of its objectives "the granting of special treatment to member states classified in favour of land-locked, semi-landlocked, and Island countries".

Notwithstanding that most of the present co-operation efforts emphasise trade liberalisation, the existing integration processes are better than the principle of standing alone.

The African Economic Treaty and other regional bodies

The African Economic Treaty represents continental effort at integration. There are however other regional bodies such as the Economic Community of West African States (ECOWAS), the East African Community (EAC), the South African Development Co-ordination Conference (SADCC) and the Preferential Trade Area (PTA).

The African Economic Treaty

The African Economic Treaty was signed in Lagos on the third day of June 1991. It was the end product of so many years of conception. The fifty-one African States are members of this continental body.

The Treaty is made up of one hundred and six Articles. The projected period for the realisation of its objectives is thirty four years. The objectives of the Treaty could be summarised as follows:
  (a) Promotion of collective, accelerated, self-reliant and self-sustaining development;

---

[7] The preamble to the African Economic Treaty states that the African Economic Community shall constitute an integral part of the OAU. Article 99 further provides that the AET Treaty and the Protocols shall form an integral part of the OAU Charter.

(b) Promotion of co-operation among African States and integration in all the economic, social and cultural fields.

For the purpose of achieving these objectives, six stages of varying duration all amounting to thirty four years have been outlined. The stages are:[8]

Stage 1: Strengthening of regional economic communities of member states and establishment of others where they do not yet exist. This is to take five years.

Stage 2: Taking of the following measures at regional level - stabilisation of tariff and non-tariff barriers, customs duty and other similar taxes and local taxes; elimination of tariff and non-tariff barriers and harmonisation of customs duty and similar taxes vis-à-vis third party states; strengthening sectoral integration on the regional and continental levels; co-ordination and harmonisation of activities among regional economic communities. Eight years have been earmarked for the achievement of these aims.

Stage 3: Each regional economic community is enjoined to establish a free trade zone to be followed by the setting up of a customs union through the adoption of a common external tariff. This is to take ten years.

Stage 4: The next two years after the third stage is for co-ordination and harmonisation of tariff and non-tariff systems by the regional economic communities for the purpose of setting up a customs union at the continental level.

Stage 5: After the establishment of a continental customs unions, the next envisaged achievement is an African common market through the adoption of relevant measures for such a market in fields such as agriculture, transport, communications, energy and scientific research. The Treaty also envisages during this

---

[8] *The African Economic Community - The Destiny of a continent,* a publication of the Organisation of African Unity pp18-20.

period harmonisation of monetary, financial and fiscal policies, free movement of persons, right of residence and establishment and the constitution of community resources. The above is to be achieved within four years.

Stage 6: This is the last stage in the series. This period is to last for five years. During this period, the gains of the Common Market will be consolidated and strengthened: this stage also envisages free movement of persons, goods and capital and application of the right of residence and establishment. During this period also, all sectors are to be integrated. Other things which are expected to be done during this stage are the establishment of an African Monetary Fund, a Central Bank and a single currency. Steps will also be taken to complete the institution of the structure of the Pan-African Parliament whose members shall be elected by universal suffrage; the process of harmonisation and co-ordination of the activities of regional economic communities; the establishment of structures for multinational enterprises and the executive organs of the Community.

The Treaty envisages the possibility of not achieving all the aims ascribed to a particular period within the stated time frame, hence it provides that the Assembly, on the recommendation of the Council, shall confirm that the objectives of a particular stage have been attained and shall approve the transition to the next stage. But notwithstanding this provision, the Treaty does not permit the cummulative transitional period to exceed forty (40) years from the date of entry into force of this Treaty.[9]

For the purpose of achieving these objectives certain organs of the community have been established.[10] The Assembly of Heads of State and Government constitutes the supreme organ of the Community.[11]

---

[9] Article 5 (5)
[10] Article 7 of the Treaty
[11] Article 8

The Treaty enjoins the Assembly to meet once a year in regular session.[12] It is also to act by decisions.[13] There shall also be established a Pan-African Parliament[14] and a Court of Justice of the Community.[15] The decisions of the court of Justice shall be binding on Member States and organs of the Community.[16]

The Treaty encourages free movement of persons, right of residence and establishment.[17] The Treaty also takes care of least developed, landlocked, semi-landlocked and Island countries.[18]

The objectives of the Treaty are laudable. These objectives can be achieved with a lot of sincerity and common will. No meaningful economic or political co-existence can be achieved at the continental level without the will to submit part of each nation's sovereignty and or power. A common market, free movement of persons, goods, services and capital are essential requirements in any economic union. A unified monetary system and harmonious economic, social and cultural policies and values of member states of such a union are also essential. The laudable objectives highlighted above ought to be enthusiastically pursued by all nations that are forward looking.

Regional economic communities

Despite the establishment of the African Economic Treaty, regional economic communities still exist. Indeed, the Treaty calls for the strengthening of existing economic communities and the establishment of such communities in other regions of Africa.

Various roles have been assigned to the regional economic communities. They are relevant in five of the six stages highlighted by

---

[12] Article 9
[13] Article 10
[14] Article 14
[15] Article 18
[16] Article 19
[17] Article 43
[18] Article 79

the Treaty.[19] The said roles range from strengthening and coordinating their activities, to the establishment of a free trade zone among member states, the establishment of a customs union which will eventually lead to the lifting of custom barriers with the result that customs tariffs, quota restrictions or prohibitions as well as non-tariff barriers will be eliminated.

Emphasising the relations which should exist between the Community and regional economic communities, the Treaty provides that decisions of the Assembly are binding on both member states and organs of the community as well regional economic communities. Apart from the regional economic communities, the African Economic Treaty enjoins the community to establish close relations with other African organisations, socio-economic associations and international organisations.

The economic community of West African states

The Treaty of the Economic Community of West African States (ECOWAS) was signed on the 28th day of May 1975 following the signing of the Treaty by fifteen of the Heads of State and Government of West African States.[20] It came into operation on 10th June 1975 when seven signatory states ratified the Treaty. It must however be stated that ECOWAS did not become operational till the beginning of 1977.

Like any supra state economic set-up, ECOWAS arose out of the genuine desire to examine and eliminate inconsistencies and obstacles on the part of the states constituting this body towards the main objective of building as rapidly and smoothly as possible, a harmonious

---

[19] Article 6

[20] The states were Nigeria, Togo, Liberia, Ghana, Upper Volta, Guinea, Ivory Coast, Gambia, Sierra Leone, Niger, Benin Republic, Guinea Bissau, Mauritania, Mali and Senegal. The Republic of Cape Verde later joined as the sixteenth member state.

and unified community on the basis of economic integration in the West African region.[21]

West Africa is made up of a land area of about 6,415,401 square kilometres and a population of about 110 million people. The population has been on the increase. Commercial crops like tropical oils, groundnut and coffee can be found in large quantities and 60% of the world's cocoa[22] can be found within this geographical conglomerate called West Africa. Other mineral resources like Iron Ore, Bauxite, Copper, Tin, Columbite, Diamond, Gold, Manganese and Petroleum can also be found in this region. Unfortunately however, despite the natural endowments, this region is one of those beset by poverty and squalor by reason of underdevelopment and other human induced problems.

From the above, it would be discovered that there is the need to increase intra-trade relationship not only between the West African States but also among the African countries. There is therefore, the need to examine the ECOWAS Treaty, but before this is embarked upon, it should be stated that the fact that not much trading could be recorded among the West African nations means that much needs to be done in relation to the unity which the ECOWAS forum provides and by necessary implication the African Economic Treaty.

Analysis of the ECOWAS Treaty

The ECOWAS Treaty which was signed in Lagos on 28 May 1975 has been revised. The Revised Treaty was signed on the 24th day of July 1993. [23] The basic objective of the community could be found in Article 3 which states:

> The aims of the Community are to promote co-operation and integration, leading to the establishment of an economic union in

---

[21] Alhaji Momodu Munu - *Ten Years of ECOWAS* 1975 - 1985 published by the ECOWAS Secretariat Lagos, June 1985.

[22] See *The Atlas of Africa*, New York, The Free Press 1975 pp. 111-113.

[23] See the Revised Treaty of ECOWAS

West Africa in order to raise the living standards of its peoples, and to maintain and enhance economic stability, foster relations among member states and contribute to the progress and development of the African Continent.

For the purpose of achieving these objectives, the Treaty provides that the community shall by stages ensure the following, [24] *among others*:

i.   the harmonisation and co-ordination of national policies and the promotion of integration programmes, projects and activities, particularly in food, agriculture and natural resources, industry, transport and communication, energy, trade, technology and legal matters.

ii. The establishment of a common market through

   (a) the liberalisation of trade by the abolition, among member states of customs duties levied on imports and exports, and the abolition, among member states, of non-tariff barriers in order to establish a free trade area at the Community level.

   (b) the adoption of a common external tariff and a common trade policy vis-à-vis third countries.

   (c) the removal, between member states, of obstacles to the free movement of persons, goods, services and capital, and to the right of residence and establishment.

   (d) the establishment of an economic union through the adoption of common policies in the economic, financial, social and cultural sectors, and the creation of a monetary union.

   (e) the promotion of balanced development of the region, paying attention to the special problems of each member state particularly those of landlocked and small island member states.

An important objective of the community is the harmonisation and co-ordination of national policies and the promotion of integration programmes. Much could be achieved if this objective is faithfully

---

[24] See Article 3.

followed. There would be less divergence in the policies of member states. The problem however is that since the inception of ECOWAS little has been done to achieve this objective. Each nation goes its own way in respect of the policies it decides to pursue. The problem becomes more pronounced because of lack of commitment to implement many of the protocols of the community. National interest is often sacrificed on the altar of sheer adherence to national sovereignty since harmonisation and co-ordination in this respect have issues like food production, improvement in agricultural activities, positive use of natural resources, improvement in transport and communication as well as technological advancement and uniform or harmonious legal matters in focus, lack of commitment to harmonise or co-ordinate activities in this respect would definitely have a perilous effect on the aims and objectives of the community.

Another important objective of the community is co-operation in trade, customs, taxation, statistics, money and payments. Article 35 provides for the establishment of a customs union within a maximum period of fifteen (15) years following the commencement of the regional trade liberalisation scheme adopted by the Authority through its Decision A/Dec. 1/9/83 of 20 May, 1983 and launched on 1 January, 1990.[25] It should however be stated that given the uneven levels of development in the region, some states may lose revenue by reason of trade liberalisation. Article 48 provides for compensation for loss of revenue arising from trade liberalisation. It must also be stated that some of the West African states are seemingly inextricably attached to their former colonial masters. Indeed, the initial problem of ECOWAS was how to bring in and enjoy the loyalty and confidence of the French speaking West African states that were seemingly inextricably attached to France, their former colonial master. It should also be stated that the reduction and elimination of tariffs, taxes and duties on intra-community goods and the pursuit of common external tariff toward third parties

---

[25] Article 54 Revised ECOWAS Treaty.

often lead to reduced national earnings which then tend to affect member states differently.[26]

This objective also closes its eyes to the political wranglings among the African states. For example, Nigeria expelled millions of ECOWAS citizens in 1985 because they were declared illegal aliens, yet the community Treaty envisages removal between member states of obstacles to the free movement of persons, goods, services and capital and to the right of residence and establishment. Frequent closure of borders between neighbouring states is also a common phenomenon.

There are also provisions relating to the institutions of the Community. The Authority of Heads of State and Government of member states is the supreme institution of the community. This body is responsible for the general direction and control of the Community. The Authority acts by decisions. Under it is the Council of Ministers which is comprised of the Minister in charge of ECOWAS Affairs and any other Minister of each member state. The Council acts by Regulations. The Executive Secretary heads the secretariat. Seven Commissions have also been established. The Treaty also establishes a court of Justice for the community.

Article 84 allows Members States to enter into agreements among themselves and with non-member states, regional organisations or any other international organisation, provided that economic agreements in this respect are not incompatible with the provisions of the Treaty. Where the agreements entered into before the entry into force of the Treaty between Member states and non-member states, regional organisations or any other international organisations are incompatible with the provisions of this Treaty, the Member or Member states concerned shall take appropriate measures to eliminate such incompatibility.[27] This is a laudable objective, but whether it would be observed in practice is another matter entirely. Moreover, it is doubtful whether the existing framework can achieve this objective. The Revised ECOWAS Treaty takes care of the defects inherent in the 1975 Treaty.

---

[26] Ibrahim Gambari *op cit.*
[27] Article84 of the Revised ECOWAS Treaty

For example, under the new Treaty, the power of the ECOWAS Authority of Heads of State and Government has been highlighted, [28] so is the ECOWAS Council of Ministers.[29] It also takes care of the binding effect of the decisions of the Community's court of Justice.[30]

The East African community

This Community consisted of Kenya, Tanzania and Uganda. It was once the most advanced regional integration scheme in Africa.[31] The official language of the Community is English. Swahili is the local language that is more widely spoken throughout the region. It covers a land area of about 1.76 million square kilometres. Thus regional economic integration scheme was started by and for the convenience of the colonial power, Britain.[32] According to Brett[33]during the colonial period, Kenya became an economically viable European white community in East Africa. Uganda was a protectorate and Tangayika a trust territory. The economies of these two countries were subordinated to the needs and priorities of the white settlers in Kenya. The result was the discouragement of an indigenous entrepreneurial class in East Africa especially in Uganda and Tanzania. The infrastructures favoured Kenya. Gambari giving account of this development said:

> Skewed as it may have been in favour of the settler community in Kenya, economic co-operation was an early fact of life in the sub-region. In 1917, the Kenyan and Ugandan protectorates merged their customs authorities. Common tariff rates between Kenya and

---

[28] Article 7

[29] Article 10

[30] Article 76. See also Kofi Oteng Kufuor: "Critical Issues Arising out of the New ECOWAS Treaty" 1994 Vol. 4 pt. 3 *AJICL* pp. 432-433.

[31] It has even been opined that the EAC's effort was the most advanced regional idea at integration in the whole of the developing world

[32] Ibrahim A. Gambari Ibid. p. 33

[33] Brett E.A., *Colonialism and Under-development in East Africa - The Politics of Economic Change,* 1919 - 1939 (New York: Non Publishers 1973)

Uganda were also extended to Tangayika (Tanzania) in 1922. By the following year, the three territories engaged in free trade for local produce. This was followed in 1972 by an agreement which removed almost all customs duties between the three territories. Also, by that time, East Africa operated in a system of common currency with the introduction of the East African shilling, issued by a sub-regional currency board.[34]

The above scenario must have impelled then President Julius K. Nyerere to write in March 1963:

> A federation of at least Kenya, Uganda and Tangayika (Tanzania) should be comparatively easy to achieve. We already have a common market, and run many services through the Common Services Organisation - which has its own Central Legislative Assembly and an executive composed of the Prime Ministers of the three states. This is the nucleus from which a federation is the natural growth.[35]

The dream of Nyerere could however not be realised. This arose from various factors which include lopsidedness in the distribution of costs and benefits. While Kenya was considered favoured, others felt cheated. Secondly, the three members of the community differed ideologically. Kenya basically structured its economy on capitalist model and at independence adopted mixed economy. Tanzania followed the socialist orientation of President Nyerere. In relation to Uganda, the rudderless regime of Idi Amin did not give the country a clear vision. Given the above political and social systems it was difficult to operate a common market. Furthermore, the East African Community Treaty had as its focus the "transfer tax system". This became contentious and inadequate as the basis for solving the industrial gap created by the lopsided development created which favoured Kenya. The above factors,

---

[34] Ibrahim Gambari Ibid. p. 69
[35] Rothchild D.; *Politics of Integration - An East African Documentary* p. 1 See also "A United States of Africa" *Journal of Modern African Studies* Vol. 1 No. 1 (March 1963) pp. 5-6.

in the main, led to the dismantling of the East African Community Treaty.

It should however be stated that moves are being made for the resuscitation of the Community. There are reports that between 23rd and 24th January 1994, Kenya, Tanzania and Uganda held a ministerial mediation meeting in Nairobi which led to the signing of the East African Community Mediation Agreement. During the meeting, the age long dispute relating to the assets and liabilities of the defunct East African Community was amicably settled.[36]

The above gave the East African Community Mediation Co-ordination Committee the impetus to continue its reconciliatory talks in Nairobi. Following the above, the presidents of Kenya, Tanzania and Uganda signed an agreement for further and better co-operation in Arusha, Tanzania on the 30th of November, 1993. The Permanent Tripartite Commission (PTC) of Ministers took place on the 12th March 1996 following the reactivation of the Treaty for East African co-operation in Kampala, Uganda on November 26th 1994. At the major summit of Heads of State meeting which was held on 13th March 1996 Ambassador Francis K. Muthaura of Kenya was appointed as the executive secretary for the East African Community. It is hoped that this new impetus will give the community the necessary vigour for the actualisation of its aims and objectives.[37]

---

[36] Owasanoye B. O. and Yagba T. A. T. "The Changing Obligations Arising from National and Sub-regional International Legal Treaties and Instrument Relating to Migration and their Integration in National Law and Administrative Practice" (Unpublished 1996). According to them, the information in relation to the resuscitation of the Community was supplied by Mr. David Ketogho, Second Secretary, Kenyan High Commission, Lagos, Nigeria.

[37] Owosanoye B. O. and Yagba T. A. T. *op cit.*

The South African Development Co-ordination Conference (SADCC)/Southern African Development Community (SADC)

With the emergence of countries like Angola and Mozambique as independent states and the liberation struggles in other South African States, the need for integration became necessary. It even became very pertinent given the apartheid rule in South Africa. The Front Line States made up of Angola, Mozambique, Botswana, Zambia and Tanzania and later Lesotho, Malawi, Swaziland and Zimbabwe signed the Lusaka Declaration on Economic Liberation which led to the emergence of the South African Development Co-ordination Conference (SADCC) on April 1, 1980. The cautionary step taken by the founding fathers of SADDC are:

(a) The reduction of economic dependence, particularly but not only, on the Republic of South Africa.

(b) The forging of links to create a genuine and equitable regional integration.

(c) The mobilisation of resources to promote the implementation of national interstate and regional policies, and

(d) concerted action to secure international co-operation within the framework of SADCC strategy for economic liberation.[38]

From the above, it could be deduced that SADCC was averse to economic domination by South Africa. Unlike other economic bodies, SADCC avoided a common-market approach. It adopts instead a "national decision-making" approach. President Dos Santos, stated the basic intention of SADCC at its seventh Summit in Lusaka. He said:

> When the nine countries of the region came together in this capital in 1980, thus realising the genial idea of the late President Seretse Khama by signing the Lusaka Declaration, we were perfectly aware that we were not creating an organisation that would integrate the economies of our countries into a conventional

---

[38] Ibrahim A. Gambari Ibid. p. 85.

community system. We were aware that we would not immediately aspire to a model of organisation that would defend us from international competition and would favour inter-regional trade because we do not possess an industrial infrastructure that would compete in the external market, nor do we possess immediate means for developing a system of inter-regional trade.[39]

The following could be said to be the consequences of the above stated objective:

(i) Reliance on external financial assistance for the execution of specific projects in individual member states. The annual consultative conference which could be attended by donor bodies was satisfactory to such bodies as they could express their views and preferences during the Conference.

(ii) Since the co-operation was a loose one, its institutional mechanism was small and inexpensive.

(iii) This body also became the instrument for ensuring and enhancing the national security of member states.

(iv) Since political issues played a relatively small part, ideological differences did not cause much friction.

It should however be stated that the SADCC cannot run away from a common market strategy since inter-state trade is a positive development in any regional community.

In July 1998, trade was added as an area of co-operation. The responsibility for the trade programme together with the co-ordination of the industrial sector was allocated to Tanzania. The independence of South Africa has given a new impetus to the South African Co-operation.

The integration effort in the Southern part of Africa has taken a new dimension following the independence of the Republic of South Africa from white domination or apartheid. The body is now known as Southern African Development Community following the admission of

---

[39] Reported in "FBS, Inter-African Affairs VIII" (Washington D. C., July 27, 1987) p. BB2 and cited in Ibrahim Gambari ibid. p. 86.

South Africa as member in 1992. The objectives of the Treaty establishing this community are:

(a) Deeper economic co-operation and integration on the basis of balance, equality and mutual benefits, cross border investment and trade, freer movement of factors of production, goods and services across national boundaries.

(b) Common economic, political and social values and systems, enhancing enterprise, competitiveness, democracy and good governance, respect for the rule of law and human rights, alleviation of poverty; and

(c) Strengthened regional solidarity, peace and security for the purpose of advancing harmony.

The Preferential Trade Area (PTA)

This body comprises some Eastern and South African states. It was formed in 1981. The objective is to improve commercial and economic co-operation in the region and to transform the structure of production of national economies in the region. Other aims are promotion of regional trade, creation of institutional bodies to facilitate trade and industry, promotion of agricultural development and improved transportation links. Members of this body are Namibia, Mozambique, Mauritius, Rwanda, Somalia, Uganda, Zambia, Zimbabwe, Tanzania, Swaziland, Angola, The Comoros, Djibouti, Ethiopia, Burundi, Botswana, Kenya, Lesotho and Malawi. It should be stated that despite the fact that many of the members of SADCC are also members of the PTA, the two bodies presently co-exist. This body aims to establish a common market by the year 2000.

Probable areas of conflict and difficulties between the African Economic Treaty and the regional bodies

The Preamble to the African Economic Treaty notes the efforts already made in continental and regional sectoral economic co-operation, and the encouragement which it brings. It consequently states that there is justification in having a larger and fuller economic integration. Indeed, the first stage of the Treaty[41] calls for strengthening of existing regional economic communities and within a period not exceeding five years from the date of entry into force of the Treaty, the establishment of economic communities in regions where they are yet to exist.

It should be noted that many of these regional bodies have been in existence before the signing of the African Economic Treaty. Some of the aims and objectives of these bodies do not tally with those of the African Economic Treaty. The Treaty however enjoins these bodies to harmonise their activities and bring them in line with those of the AET. This could be gathered from Article 28(2) of the AET which provides that:

> Member states shall take all necessary measures aimed at progressively promoting increasingly closer co-operation among the communities, particularly through co-ordination and harmonisation of their activities in all fields or sectors in order to ensure the realisation of the objectives of he community.

Ordinarily, the AET should be regarded as the parent body in the harmonisation or co-operative process among the African nations. It seems however that to say this, without more, is to adopt a simplistic approach to the complex commercial process in Africa. It seems doubtful that a nation or a region will willingly surrender a project or an economic activity which it considers dear to it just because it conflicts with the continental objective. Furthermore, in some countries, Treaties do not take the form of law until such Treaties are ratified by the domestic legislative body.[42] Self Preservation might be the first law. The situation becomes more complex if it is realised that despite Article 28, Article 29 encourages at the second stage, the recognition of discriminatory customs duties, quota restrictions, other restrictions or prohibition of the issues contained in Article 29. A rigid adherence to the provisions of a regional objective may thwart the laudable

---

[41] Article 5 of the AET Treaty

[42] See Section 12 of the 1979 Constitution which requires that Treaties entered into by Nigeria should be ratified by the National Assembly.

continental objective which the AET hopes to achieve in the final analysis. For example, while the original ECOWAS Treaty did not have the AET as a specific continental body in mind, it mentions it specifically in Article 78 of the Revised Treaty and states that the integration of the region shall constitute an essential component of the integration of the African Continent. It enjoins member states to undertake to facilitate the co-ordination and harmonisation of the policies and programmes of the community with those of the African Economic Community.

The laudable objectives of the AET can only be achieved in a harmonious environment. Political instability is an order of the day in Africa. There is the incessant accusation of one country encouraging the overthrow of the government of its neighbouring state. It therefore seems improbable that a conducive economic atmosphere will be achieved in the face of incessant political instability, and intra-regional suspicion. For example, SADCC came into being for the purpose of discouraging economic dependence on the Republic of South Africa. Prior to the dismantling of apartheid, it was impossible to bring South Africa as a member of the SADCC. Furthermore, between Nigeria and Benin Republic, there are not less than ten border posts. The above may impede free flow of trade and inter-state confidence.

The African Economic Treaty and some of the regional groupings have as their objective trade liberalisation. It could, however, not be said that all the regional bodies in Africa have trade liberalisation as their objective. For example, at inception, the South African Development Co-ordination Conference (SADCC) avoided a common-market approach or trade. As President Santos put it, the intention was not to aspire to a model of organisation that would defend the body from international competition or the one that favoured inter-regional trade.[43] With the emergence of SADC and President Mandela at the helm of affairs, it is hoped that much will be achieved in the area of common-

---

[43] This is also one of the problems besetting harmonisation or integrative efforts among the Latin American States. See also *Regionalism and The World Trading System* published by World Trade Organisation April, 1995.

market, if not at the level of SADC, it should be achieved on the floor of the AET.

The allegiance between member states of the various regional bodies and organisations impede total commitment and unalloyed loyalty to the continental integration efforts. Until these economic co-operation arrangements are rationalised and harmonised the competing and conflicting claims and commitments on member states to these diverse bodies and interest groups will continue to dissipate the envisaged dynamism of integration efforts. Furthermore, even within a sub-regional grouping there may also exist sub-divisions. An example is the separate union of French speaking West African Countries within the ECOWAS.

Divergence in the institutional arrangement between the AET and other regional bodies may be a source of conflict. It is necessary to study and determine the institutions that can bring about unity or that will be in line with the aims and objectives of the various economic unions and the AET.

There are various legal systems in Africa. A virile integration effort requires a settled legal system as this would promote commerce. There is however a legal gulf between the civil law and common law systems in Africa. Legal scholars from both systems rarely interact, there is little or no effort to harmonise the legal systems in Africa.[44] Indeed, there has been little effort to achieve this at regional level. Article 18 of the AET which deals with the court of Justice merely states that a court of Justice of the Community shall be constituted. It does not say anything about harmonisation of laws in Africa. What is more appalling is that Article 25 which lists the Specialised Technical Committees fails to establish a committee on Law. This body would have been able to harmonise the legal systems in Africa and bring out harmonious rules for the purpose of achieving the objectives of the AET. Furthermore, the Treaty does not state whether there should be any hierarchical link between the courts of the regional bodies and the one to be established by the AET. For example, in respect of ECOWAS, the Revised Treaty states in Article 76

---

[44] Ibrahim Gambari, ibid.

that any dispute regarding the interpretation or the application of the provisions of the Treaty shall be amicably settled through direct agreement without prejudice to the provisions of the Treaty and relevant Protocols. Failing this, either party or any other member state or the Authority may refer the matter to the Court of the Community whose decision shall be final and shall not be subject to appeal. One interpretation of this provision is that this court is the final court in respect of all issues that fall to be determined under the ECOWAS Treaty, but there is another side to this argument. Assuming that the AET reaches it's third or fourth stage, and a particular issue that deals with trade liberalisation is transferred to the continental body having regard to the requirement that regional bodies should co-ordinate, harmonise, and eliminate divergent trade liberalisation and customs issues, such issues must of necessity become continental matters. If there is a dispute as regards the interpretation or implementation of any matter touching on the customs unions or trade liberalisation, which court shall have jurisdiction? Should it be the court established by the AET? Can't the court established by ECOWAS, for example, serve as a court of first instance in a trade liberalisation issue emanating from West Africa and that established by the continental body be an appellate court. What shall be the legal status of decisions emanating from neighbouring regional bodies on similar issues in a regional forum court. Except there is a provision for a hierarchical link, the issue of the relationship between the court established by the regional body and the continental body might be a matter of conjecture. It is interesting to note that Article 57 of the Revised ECOWAS Treaty enjoins member states to undertake to co-operate in judicial and legal matters with a view to harmonising their judicial and legal systems. There is also a Technical Commission established by the Revised ECOWAS Treaty on Judicial and Legal Affairs.

Some of the member states may also cling to their sovereignty. Where this is done, such a member state or region may not want to surrender what it may consider the economic autonomy which goes with its sovereignty.

One of the things that led to the death of the East African Community was the lopsidedness in the siting of projects. Kenya, which was an economically viable European white community enjoyed the basic amenities commensurate with the British way of life. The other members of the Community - Tanzania and Uganda felt cheated. Various methods adopted to correct this development did not work. This therefore served as one of the reasons why the East African Community union died. Given this fact, it is necessary for the regional bodies and the AET to ensure equitable location of institutions and provisions of amenities among the member states.

Refusal of member states or regional bodies to honour their financial obligations may cripple the union. It is therefore necessary for member states to fulfil their financial commitments.

Article 5 (4) of the AET Treaty states that the transition from one stage to another shall be determined when the specific objectives set in the Treaty or pronounced by the Assembly for a particular stage are implemented and all commitments fulfilled. The problem with this provision is that the objective set for a particular phase may conflict with that set for a phase in the Treaty of a region. It may therefore be difficult to bring the objective of the AET within the framework of the region at the time stipulated by the AET.

There is no uniform currency in Africa. Most of the currencies are not even convertible. The East African Community has an edge over ECOWAS in respect of uniformity of currencies. The three partner states have long been using one currency - the Pound Sterling. [45] The same cannot be said of the ECOWAS States where there are various currencies. The French member states of ECOWAS belong to the West African Monetary Union (UMOA) with a common Central Bank - BCEAO. The realisation of the need to have a common currency led to the formation of West African Central Banks (AWACH) and now the West African Clearing House (WACH) which was launched on 1 July 1976. A common currency that transcends regional boundaries is a *sine qua non* to prevent frictions or difficulties inherent in using various

---

[45] **Article 87** of the Revised ECOWAS Treaty.

currencies. It is doubtful whether member states' resort to the use of intervention currencies can solve the problem that is being highlighted here.

The influence of former colonial overlords should also be considered. One of the reasons why the French speaking West African countries did not want to join ECOWAS initially was the continuing network of cultural, educational, economic and military ties they had with France. All member states of the regions and AET should have the assurance of adequate assistance and protection in times of need otherwise the region or member state in need will turn its back to the continental integration and look up to its former colonial master. Such a region may consider its colonial master that decides to help it in time of need its friend indeed.

Another problem which may affect the progressive working relationship between the regional bodies and the AET is the problem of language. In relation to East African Community, the fact that the East African Common Market shared a common colonial experience under the British made it possible for them to have English Language as their official language. Swahili is also the common local language. The same cannot be said of the ECOWAS states which were former British, French and Portuguese colonies with the attendant divergent official languages, administrative structure, and educational systems. Indeed, the Revised Treaty of ECOWAS states that the official languages of the community shall be all West African languages so designated by the Authority as well as English, French and Portuguese. [46] This factor can bring about difficulty in the attainment of the objectives of the regional groups and the AET.

It should also be noted that a consensus on liberalisation is easier to achieve among a small group of like-minded countries than among the greater number of countries.

---

[46] See Akinyemi A. A. and Aloko I. A. *Readings and Documents on ECOWAS.* Simai M and Caram K., (Ed.) *Economic International concepts, Theories and Problems.*

A peep into the future

The hitherto discussion reveals that integration process constitutes a chain of activities and responsibilities which are usually couched in terms of objectives, the decision making organ, institutions, the member states and the external development partners.

The age-long activities at co-operation at regional level point to the aspirations of many of our people to be beneficiaries of some of the basic things which are better achieved or attained through concerted efforts. The journey may not have been smooth sailing but its tortuous nature should not diminish the stature of integration efforts at supra national level. The various regional bodies may have different histories but the end which each attempted and still attempts to achieve can be brought together. The recent effort at continental groupings among the African nations bears eloquent testimony to the belief in unity in diversity. Now that the African Economic Treaty is in place with adequate accommodation for regional interests, there is the need to take a peep into the future for the purpose of bringing to view how the objectives of the regional bodies and the AET can be achieved for the purpose of bringing about regional and continental wealth and law, which is a method of social engineering can definitely bring this to pass. The above can be achieved notwithstanding the seemingly teething problems highlighted above. It is in consequence of the above that the followings are hereby suggested:

(a) Trade liberalisation *per se* is not enough, there is the need to develop an integrated physical infrastructure to ensure cohesion and economic development. The economic groupings should therefore not exist merely as instruments for the establishment of free trade areas.

(b) Strict quota system should be discouraged both at the continental and regional levels for staff recruitment. The contrary will lead to undue politicisation of appointments. The relevant community will therefore be saddled with unqualified or sub-standard professional personnel. The aims and objectives of any community can only be achieved where the community is managed by competent hands.

(c) The existing inadequate institutional arrangements should be corrected. For example, the relationship between the regional judicial systems and the AET should be stated especially in relation to the relationship between the regional courts and the court established by the AET.

(d) There is the need to create a single currency for Africa. This would definitely promote free flow of trade.

(e) At the regional level, there is the need to decentralise some aspects of the co-operation programmes by which the responsibility of the execution or implementation of sectoral programmes could be assigned to specific member states.

(f) By this method, there could be a scheme that would be centrally controlled but responsibility for implementation will be given to particular states.

(g) Any union requires good faith and deep sense of purpose, there should therefore be willingness on the part of members of the groupings to comply with and implement community policies and programmes.

(h) There should be a convergence of legal systems. The divergent legal systems instead of being a problem should enrich not only the legal systems of regional groupings but also the continental body (the AET).

(i) There is the need to surrender some measure of sovereignty by member states so as to be able to achieve the success attributable to integrative schemes.

(j) All measures that impede the free movement of persons, services and capital should be removed.

(k) The African Economic Treaty and the regional bodies should maintain cordial relationship with the EEC and other regional bodies outside Africa.

(l) There is lack of basic statistical data on the problems and achievements of the existing regional bodies. It is therefore difficult to assess the achievements of these bodies. There is therefore the need to provide basic statistical data upon which the probable repercussions of regional integration can be assessed.

(m) There is the need to put to an end the wasteful practice in which each country concentrates on its own development regardless of what its neighbour is doing.

(h) The African Economic Treaty should have adequate provisions which could facilitate the use of regional groupings as viable channels for launching regional programmes. Conducive environment which would encourage donation from relevant and willing agencies should be provided.

(o) Private organisations or companies should also be encouraged to invest. A conducive atmosphere should be provided in order to facilitate the realisation of this objective.

(p) The hoe and cutlass are still the basic tillage implements. It is impossible to achieve the envisaged agricultural development at any level with the above tools. There is therefore the need to improve on our technology for the purpose of harvesting and putting to good use the agricultural products with which the continent is blessed.

(q) It is necessary to have a mutual display of trust on the part of members of the regional bodies and the AET. This cannot be wished away in our efforts at integration.

(r) There is the need to avoid the temptation of sacrificing long-term benefits for short-term gains.

(s) There is also the need for member states to display some measure of maturity. Ability to absorb some economic shock or non-realisation of a given objective should not put an end to the need to join the progressive vehicle of integration.

The trend towards the formation and strengthening of various regional and continental groupings is an indication of the universal awareness of the interdependence of mankind on economic issues and other matters necessary for human interaction or co-existence.[47]

---

[47] Simai M. and Garam K. (Ed.), *Economic Integration: Concepts, Theories and Problems*, ibid. p. 41. A Yoruba (A tribe In Nigeria) proverb says "Agbajo owo la fi nsoya". It means that a lot can be achieved through unity. The same can be said of integration efforts. See also Alhaji M. I. Yahaya, "African Regional Economic Integration: Issues and Development" *Union Digest*, Vol. 4, Nos. 2 and 3, September, 1998, pp. 4-13.

Selected articles

Chen, "Private International Law of the People's Republic of China: An Overview" (1987) 35 *Am J. Comp. L.* 445.

De Nova R., "Historical and Comparative Introduction to Conflict of Laws" (1966) *Recueil des cours* vol. 11 443

De Nova R., "The First American Book on Conflict of Laws" (1964) *Am. J. Legal Hist.* 135.

Dowrick F.E., "Juristic Activity in the Council of Europe - 25th Year" (1994) 23 *I.C.L.Q* 610.

Gabor, "A Socialist Approach to Codification of Private International Law in Hungary: Comments and Translation" (1980) 55 *Tul. L. Rev.* 63.

Garro A.M., "Unification and Harmonisation of Private Law in Latin America" (1992) 40 *Am. J. Comp. L.* 587.

Juenger, "American and European Conflicts Law" (1982) 30 *Am.J. Comp. L.* 117.

Juenger, "The Conflicts Statute of the German Democratic Republic: An Introduction and Translation" (1977) 25 *Am. J. Comp. L.* 332.

Koopmans T., "The Birth of European Law at the Crossroads of Legal Traditions" (1991) 39 *Am. J. Comp. L.* 493.

Kufuor O.K., "Critical Issues Arising Out of the New ECOWAS Treaty" (1994) Vol.4 pt.3 *AJICL* 432.

Lando O., "Principles of European Legislation" (1992) 40 *Am. J. Comp. L.* 573.

Mcdougal L. III, "Private International Law: *Ius Gentium* Versus Choice of Law Rules or Approaches" (1990) 38 *Am. J. Comp. L.* 521.

Morse C.G.J., Choice of Law in Tort: A Comparative Survey (1984) 32 *Am. J. Comp. L.* 51.

Nadelmann, Watchter's Essays on the Collision of Private Laws of Different States (1963) 13 *Am. J. Comp.* L. 414.

Palmer, "The Austrian Codification of Conflicts Law" (1980) 28 *Am. J. Comp. L.* 445.

Prosser, "Interstate Publication" (1953) 51 *Mich L.R.* 959

Scoles E.F., The Hague Convention on Succession (1994) *Am. J. Comp. L.* 85.

Vitta, The Impact in Europe of the American Conflicts Revolution (1982) *Am. J. Comp. L.*16.

Yntema, The Historic Bases of Private International Law (1953) 2 *Am. J. Comp. L.* 297.

Selected books

Agbede I. O., *Legal Pluralism*
Agbede I.O., *Themes on Conflict of Laws*
Ajomo M.A., *African Economic Community Treaty - Issues, Problems and Prospects.*
Ajomo M.A., *Integration of the African Continent Through Law.*
Allot A; *The Unification of Laws in Africa.*
Anton A., *Private International Law*, 2nd Ed.
Baty, *The Polarised Law*
Beale, *A Treatise on the Conflict of Laws X - XL* (1935)
Brett E.A., *Colonialism and Under-development*
Cheshire & Norths *Private International Law* (11th Ed.)
Culp M.S., *Selected Readings on Conflict of Laws*
Currie B., *Selected Essays on the Conflict of Laws.*
Dashwood R. Hacon & White R., *Guide to the Civil Jurisdiction and Judgments Convention* (1987).
Dicey A., *Digest of the Law of England with Reference to the Conflict of Laws VII* (1896)
Fletcher, *Conflict of Laws and European Community Law* (1982).
Gambari Ibrahim, *Political and Comparative Dimensions of Regional Integration - The Case of ECOWAS.*
Gibbon, *Decline and Fall of the Roman Empire CXXXXVIII.*
Harrison T., *Jurisprudence and the Conflict of Laws.*
Juenger F., *Choice of Law and Multi state Justice.*
Juenger F.K., *Private International Law*
Morris, *Conflict of Laws*
Nadelmann K. *Conflict of Laws: International and Interstate.*
Obilade A.O., *The Nigerian Legal System*
Park W., *Sources of Nigerian Law.*
Rabel, *The Conflict of Laws* (2nd ed.)
Reevs, *History of English Law.*
Rochild D., *Politics of Integration - An East African Documentary.*
Roman G.J., *Recognition and Enforcement of Foreign Judgments in Various Foreign Countries.*
Savigny V., *The Conflict of Laws*
(Guthrie's Transl.) *Sack, Conflict of Laws in the History of English Law: A*

Century of Progress 1835 - 1935.
Spiro, *Conflict of Laws.*
Sykes & Pryles, *International and Interstate Conflict of Laws.*
Webstar J.B. & Boaehen A. A., *The Growth of African Civilisation*
Wolff, *Private International Law.*